Practice Makes
PURPOSE

"Here is a book that provides practices that will awaken your heart and help us all to ventilate the world with tenderness."

Fr. Greg Boyle, S.J., Founder of Homeboy Industries, bestselling author of *Tattoos on the Heart: the Power of Boundless Compassion*

"The Six Spiritual Practices offer simple, practical tools for people who want to make a positive impact in their neighborhoods and cities."

Dan O'Neill, Founder of Mercy Corps International, bestselling author of *Signatures: the Story of John Michael Talbot*

"I found Paul's insights refreshing and thought-provoking, and would recommend this book to people in all walks of life."

Chris Dussin, Chairman of OSF International

For other resources, including the *Practice Makes PURPOSE Workbook*, a "Practice Makes PURPOSE Toolkit," and a free study guide with discussion questions for reading groups, visit www.sixpractices.com.

Practice Makes
PURPOSE

Six Spiritual Practices That Will Change
Your Life and Transform Your Community

C. Paul Schroeder

HEXAD

Published by Hexad Publishing, Minneapolis, Minnesota.

ISBN 978-0-692-83087-1
LCCN 2017901593

Cover art, design, and illustrations by Emily Crawford.
Cover photo by Addie Mannan.
Edited by Melissa Binder.

The geometric design that appears on the cover and recurs throughout the book is a universal symbol that is found in many different spiritual traditions throughout the world. It is created by superimposing six interlocking circles to create a symmetrical floral pattern. Sometimes referred to as the "flower of life," it is an image of human flourishing, unfolding to one's full potential, and as such, a visible representation of the Six Practices.

For my coworkers at New City Initiative.
You taught me more about these Six Practices
than I could say in a hundred volumes. This book
would not have been possible without you.

CONTENTS

ACKNOWLEDGMENTS

I would like to express my deep appreciation and gratitude to:

My mother Clare and my grandmother Sybil, for loving and nurturing me as a human being. My father Norm and my grandfather C.L., for teaching me how to be a man.

My wife Caroline, partner in the dance of differentiation and connection.

My children, Erin, Zach, and Lucy, and all my children and grandchildren yet to be born. You are my hope for a more compassionate and cooperative future.

The 9 Bridges Downtown Saturday Critique Meeting, for saving this project from itself on numerous occasions.

All my friends at Traditional Taekwon-Do of Portland, Oregon, who showed me what it takes to be a fighter.

Very special thanks to those without whom this book would not have been possible: Clare Schroeder (in memory of C.L. and Sybil Coward and Norman Schroeder), Chris and Tyanne Dussin, Suzeanne Mager, Kelly and John Close, Michael and Mari Lou Diamond, Bill and Pam Gates, Dan and Ann Heuvel, Ann and Jerry Hudson, J J Martin, Jan Rika Rinehart, Diana and Nick Santrizos, Tom and Donna Wehrley, and Anna E. Zeigler.

Special thanks to all who contributed to the creation of this book: Susanna Rempel, Willa Keegan-Rodewald, Dave Albertine, Richard Bahr, Melissa Binder, Matthew Boosalis, Audre Bratcher, Tom Campbell-Schmitt, Emily Crawford, Vance and Connie Hays, Jeanne Kaliszewski, John Konugres, Emily Leach, George G. Lendaris and Elizabeth Daskarolis, Christine Lentz, Matt Morris, Beth Neel, Andrea Pappajohn and Kimathi Marangu, Craig Plunkett, Deb Pratt, Rev. Stephen V. Schneider, Dave and Jean Shaffer, Jon Shaffer, Tel and Barbara Pappajohn, Kevin Scherer, Kris Soebroto and Bren Reis, Sonja Skvarla, Akira Templeton, and Judy Willis.

THE SIX SPIRITUAL PRACTICES

1. **Compassionate Seeing**
   Viewing ourselves and others with complete
   and unconditional acceptance.
   Mantra: *I accept everything I see.*

2. **Heartfelt Listening**
   Listening in such a way that our heart, our
   emotional center, is engaged and active in the
   hearing process.
   Mantra: *I hear what my heart is saying.*

3. **Intentional Welcoming**
   The ability to say no and mean it so we can say
   yes to the things that matter most to us.
   Mantra: *I honor the boundaries I set.*

4. **Joyful Sharing**
   Giving freely of ourselves without becoming
   entangled in a particular expectation or idea
   of success.
   Mantra: *I share what I have freely.*

5. **Grateful Receiving**
   Creatively reappraising our current situation
   so as to discover the gift it contains.
   Mantra: *I receive the gift that is offered.*

6. **Cooperative Building**
   Gracefully partnering with others to construct
   a new way of living together.
   Mantra: *I co-create a new reality.*

THE BASICS
The Way of the Six Practices

This is a book about how to love. Although the word "love" appears infrequently in these pages, the Six Spiritual Practices are what love looks like in action.

The world suffers more than anything else from a lack of love. The social ills that plague our neighborhoods and cities—poverty, homelessness, crime, violence—are all symptoms of this deficit. They persist because we don't love each other enough to make them stop. Such problems will not ultimately be solved by more money or social programs, though these may be necessary in the interim. They will cease through the creation of a more compassionate community.

When you engage the Six Spiritual Practices in your daily life, you are cooperating with the universe in the emergence of a new reality—a community where all people flourish.

What are the Six Spiritual Practices? They are a new formulation of a very old set of teachings and disciplines. If you apply them regularly, you will have more energy and vitality, more focus, more compassion, more clarity, and more joy. And these effects will ripple outward into your marriage and family, your parenting, your workplace, your friendships, your neighborhood and city.

These practices will change your life and transform your community. They will connect you and the people around you to Purpose, which I define as belonging to something infinitely greater than ourselves. This "something infinitely greater" is what I have in mind when I speak of "the universe" throughout this book. If you find it helpful, you can use the word "God" instead. The term we use to refer to ultimate reality is not so important. Anything real is not altered by the words we use to describe it.

The Six Practices are rooted in ancient wisdom, especially the practical, no-nonsense approach of the great spiritual masters of the Egyptian desert. More than fifteen hundred years ago, these little-known spiritual geniuses walked the path of utter simplicity, integrity, and freedom. Beyond the reach of the law or the state, they were guided only by their conscience and a few ironclad principles:

1. Never speak outside your own experience.

2. Do what works; don't do what doesn't.

3. Never judge anyone for anything.

They had no time or patience for the doctrinaire. They spoke little and taught mostly by example. Few wrote anything down; many were illiterate. Some of their sayings were eventually preserved in written form, but many came down by oral tradition alone.

The Six Spiritual Practices trace their lineage to these teachings, but they cannot be confined to any one era or religious expression. In fact, many stories from the Egyptian desert have exact parallels in the Zen tradition. They reflect the insights of modern psychology and brain science. They are timeless and universal.

Like physical training, spiritual growth does not happen instantaneously, in a moment of illumination. It requires patience, repetition, and hard work. The Six Spiritual Practices are a set of skills to be developed—not a collection of tenets you must believe in or agree to. Knowing these practices can change your life and your community doesn't lead to transformation, any more than knowing exercise benefits your heart actually improves your life span. You have to train, build up endurance, and integrate these practices into your daily life.

My Path to the Six Practices

The last thing I ever expected was to become a teacher of the Six Practices. Twenty years ago, the phrase "Six Spiritual Practices" wasn't even part of my vocabulary. The path that brought me to this point has been a winding one. I can't even say I discovered the Six Practices.

If anything, they found me.

When I was in my early twenties, restlessness and a deep desire for greater purpose drew me to the Greek Orthodox Church. I eventually went to seminary and became a priest—a role I held for more than a decade, and a vocation I believed would define my entire life. As a priest, I served at the highest levels of responsibility: archdeacon, chancellor of the local diocese, and finally dean of a cathedral parish—all by the time I turned forty.

Although I found many aspects of my work as a priest deeply satisfying, I also secretly felt constrained by the role, and I chafed at many of the restrictions. I yearned for something different, more human somehow. My spiritual journey seemed to have stalled. But by then, I was secure in my position, on a rising career path, and unwilling to make a change. I was scared of what might happen if I took a leap into the unknown, of what I might have to give up. I was afraid to jump.

So, finally, the universe gave me a push.

I fell a long, long way. My marriage of twenty years disintegrated, something I never imagined would happen until it did. Because the Orthodox tradition forbids divorce for priests, I was forced to resign from my position at the cathedral. I had the option to remain a priest, but not to continue to do the kind of work I loved. Plus, remaining a priest would mean I could never remarry. So, I made the agonizing choice to apply for laicization, release from priestly orders.

As a result of my divorce and decision to leave the priesthood, I was excommunicated and barred from attending any Greek Orthodox parish for over a year. In the span of just a few months, I had lost my marriage, my career, my priesthood, and my spiritual community—more than I had thought it was possible to lose in a lifetime.

And yet it was there, at the very lowest point of my life, that the Six Spiritual Practices appeared. This seems to be a universal pattern: you find wisdom by falling into it, like someone who stumbles headlong down a deep shaft and discovers treasure.

In my case, it happened while I was riding the bus, my only mode of transportation after giving up the car leased for me by the cathedral. I was re-reading the writings of Basil of Caesarea, one of the great spiritual masters of the Egyptian desert, whose sermons on social justice I had translated from Greek a few years earlier.

All at once, the Six Practices came to me. They simply arrived in my heart. They seemed to leap at me from the page, though Basil's teachings spoke of no such practices directly. I quickly grabbed a pencil and scribbled them down.

I had no idea at the time, but the course of my life was about to change radically.

I was captivated. The more I reflected on these practices, the more motivated I became to build a community around them. I was energized, ready to try something new and not allow fear of failure to deter me. I was finally ready to take that leap into the unknown. I started a nonprofit organization, New City Initiative, dedicated to helping people who experience poverty and homelessness realize their full human potential. I taught the Six Practices to my coworkers, and they taught them back to me in new ways and with deeper insights. Together, we taught them to many others.

New City Initiative became the "test kitchen" where the Six Spiritual Practices were tried and proved. There, I witnessed firsthand their transformative power. Volunteers told me how they had put the Six Practices to work in their marriages, their schools, and their workplaces. I began to see how they could change lives. The vignettes that appear throughout this book are inspired by their experiences.

In the end, it dawned on me: it was all a gift. The journey, the fall, the loss, the pain. All of it led to the Six Practices. It was all a gift from the universe. And every gift is given by the universe for one reason, and one reason only: to be shared.

That's why I wrote this book.

PART ONE
Compassionate Seeing

THE ISSUE
Work of Fiction

————————

There is an old story from the Egyptian desert about a monk who suspected his monastic brother of breaking the vow of celibacy. The first monk could never quite put his finger on what made him so suspicious; there was just something about the other monk that bothered him. He was constantly on the lookout for any evidence to prove his suspicions. After some surreptitious spying, he discovered the brother often slipped out of his quarters late at night, returning in the early hours before dawn.

The suspicious monk became angrier with time, listening to that creaky door night after night. He wanted justice. And so, one night, he crept out of his own quarters to follow. It was pitch black outside at first, and the other monk was nowhere to be seen. But after peering around in the darkness for a few minutes, he spotted the brother. There he was, caught in the very act with a woman, their movements half-hidden by the shadows.

His anger rose till he could stand it no more. He ran over and started kicking them, shouting, "How dare you! How long are you going to go on like this?" But by the fourth kick he'd realized his mistake: what he had thought to be two people was actually a pile of burlap sacks, animated by the shadows of tree branches waving in the moonlight.

As he stood in astonishment, a gentle voice asked, "Brother, is everything all right?" Startled, he whirled around. There, just a few yards away, he saw the other monk, his face full of concern. He was kneeling at the base of a tree, a strand of prayer beads in his hand. It was his favorite hour to pray.

How You See Determines What You See

This little story packs a powerful lesson: how you see determines *what* you see—and don't see. The suspicious monk's vision was clouded because he looked at the world through the lens of his judgments. Like him, I make judgments about other people all the time, and those judgments affect what I see in them. I hate to admit that, but it's true.

The trouble with judgments is that they prevent us from seeing clearly. Like the suspicious monk, we may end up seeing things that aren't really there. Or, we may miss things that are plain as day. This happens because we make up stories to go with our judgments—whether we intend to or not. For instance, let's say I have a new coworker named Ned who annoys me because he talks and laughs far too loudly. I assume Ned has a big ego. Almost subconsciously, my brain builds a narrative around that judgment. When I notice that Ned wears brightly patterned socks most days of the week, I consider this further proof that he's vying for attention. I don't even consider that maybe it's a subtle way for him to express creativity, or that the pop of color cheers him up on difficult mornings. No. I assume he's trying to be flashy. I fume when other team members have to raise their voices in meetings to interject an idea, and I pass harsh judgment on Ned as a husband when I notice, at the holiday party, that his wife practically has to yell to get his attention.

Four months later, Ned comes to work wearing a hearing aid. It turns out he's been slowly losing his hearing for years—and didn't know it until he finally saw a specialist.

My story explaining Ned's behavior was entirely a work of fiction.

We all create these kinds of narratives to explain others' behavior. If we're honest, it's easy to get attached to these stories—even to the point of sparking conflict. When someone says or does something that doesn't fit my story, I frequently catch myself thinking, "You are so clearly wrong on this—why can't you see it?" or "I have every right to be angry after what you did," or "If you would just take my advice on this, you'd be much better off." If a friend challenges a narrative I've built around people who support a different political candidate than I do, I might get irritated and double down on my position. I take it personally because I am invested in my story.

Over the years, I've noticed that my judgments are always reflections of my own insecurities—and I've heard this from others often enough to believe it's universal. We scoff at our neighbor's weight because we're anxious about maintaining our own. We distrust a friend's motives because we know our own to be unreliable. We roll our eyes at our loud coworker because we're obsessive about how we are perceived. We poke fun at our Type A siblings because we're ashamed of our own aimlessness. We condescend to our more laid-back colleagues for exerting less control than we do. In each case, we pin something uncomfortable about ourselves on someone else, preferring to dislike it in him or her instead. Something about the other person has tapped into our own insecurity.

This reflects another significant problem with judgments. Not only do they prevent us from seeing other people with clarity and compassion, they're symptomatic of the fact that we cannot see ourselves that way either.

This is the human dilemma in a nutshell. We make judgments based on our own insecurities, and we make up stories to support those assumptions. We believe these stories so wholeheartedly that we imagine shadows on a pile of burlap sacks to be clandestine lovers and fail to see the most obvious explanation for our coworker's decibel problem. And then, when our stories are challenged, we dig in our heels and argue with people we love.

THE FIX
Seeing You (and Me)

———

Ending the cycle of judgment requires Compassionate Seeing, the first and most fundamental of the Six Spiritual Practices. Compassionate Seeing is a moment-by-moment commitment to viewing ourselves and others with complete and unconditional acceptance—no exceptions. Here are the basic steps:

1. *Notice your discomfort.* Pay attention whenever something makes you feel uncomfortable, or seems painful, ugly, boring, or annoying. Don't try to fix or change anything. Just notice it.

2. *Suspend your judgments.* Resist the inclination to immediately decide whether something is right or wrong, or whether you like or dislike it. Don't assign blame, and don't shame yourself or anyone else.

3. *Become curious* about your experiences. Start to wonder about yourself and others. For example,

try asking, "I wonder why that bothers me so much?" or "I wonder what this is like for you?"

4. *Look deeply* with the intention to understand. Approach your experiences with a flexible mindset, and try to remain open to new information and alternative explanations.

The Two Movements of Compassionate Seeing

The First Movement: Recognizing the Difference
Compassionate Seeing has two movements, both of which are encoded in the universal spiritual prescription we know as the Golden Rule: treat others as you would want to be treated in their place. The first movement of Compassionate Seeing is *recognizing the difference* between ourselves and other people. This means seeing others as truly other—they are distinct individuals with their own unique experiences, preferences, and ambitions.

Focusing on our differences might seem counterintuitive at first, because we usually think of compassion as somehow blurring the distinction between ourselves and others. But if I don't recognize and respect the difference between me and you, I will impose my beliefs, values, and goals on you and get wrapped up in the outcome of your choices. I will act as if my story was your story, too.

Whenever I find myself trying to control other people's behavior or manage their decisions, I take it as a sign that I am having trouble separating myself from them. When I notice this is happening, I find it helpful to repeat this simple maxim to myself: "What is about you is about you, and what is about other people is about them." I have learned that as long as I keep this in mind, life tends to be much simpler for me and the people around me.

Recognizing the difference between ourselves and others is an especially critical skill when it comes to parenting. As a parent, I constantly struggle not to impose my desires and goals on my children. It's so easy for me to over-identify with them and make their success or failure about me. Much of the conflict between children and their parents happens because the parents don't recognize the difference between themselves and their children. It's important to remember always that our children have their own aspirations and life-trajectory—and they might be very different from our own.

The Second Movement: The Imaginative Leap

As we recognize and accept the difference between ourselves and others, this naturally gives rise to curiosity about their experiences. This leads us to the second movement of Compassionate Seeing: we make an *imaginative leap* across the boundary that separates us. This imaginative leap is a daring act of curiosity and creativity. Instead of imposing my values and beliefs on someone else, I begin to wonder about that person's motivations, desires, and emotions. I put myself in the other person's place, asking the question, "If I were this person in this situation, what would I think, how would I feel, and how would I want to be treated?"

As I am making an imaginative leap into someone else's situation, I notice my tendency to make judgments pauses almost automatically. Curiosity and wonder are fundamentally non-judgmental approaches to the world. I find that I simply cannot hold a judgment in my mind and be truly curious about another person at the same time. Judgments pop like soap bubbles in the presence of curiosity. As soon as I start wondering about someone else's experience, I stop selectively gathering information to support my preconceived ideas. Instead of thinking I have the other person figured out, I see that person as a mystery. Engaging a discovery mindset helps us avoid judgments and stay flexible, open, and interested.

DEEP DIVE
Seeing Through Another's Eyes

———————

Compassion is often understood in the narrow sense of identifying with people who endure misfortune or hardship. But that's only a part of what compassion is all about.

The word "compassion" comes from the Latin words *cum*, meaning "with," and *patere*, meaning "to suffer or experience"—and experiences can be pleasant, unpleasant, or neutral. So, practicing compassion actually means making a conscious and sustained effort to enter into the experience of another person, to see the world through someone else's eyes.

This means compassion is something we can practice toward everyone, not just those we consider needy or disadvantaged. We can cultivate compassion toward the rich as well as the poor, the fortunate as well as the unfortunate. And we can also cultivate compassion toward ourselves.

Compassion directed toward the self is the same

as compassion directed toward anyone else: you see yourself with complete and unconditional acceptance, you become curious about your responses and reactions, and you don't blame or shame yourself for anything. In fact, compassion for self goes hand in hand with compassion for others. If I practice negative self-talk and harsh judgment toward myself when I make a mistake, this will be my habitual response when I see someone else making the same mistake. And remember: the very qualities that irritate us the most about other people usually turn out to be the things we like least about ourselves.

For instance, if I am a quiet person, I may get quite irritated when I think other people are being too loud or rambunctious. I would never draw attention to myself by speaking so loudly, and I don't think anyone else should either. Even though I sometimes wish I could let myself go a little more, I never allow myself to stand out in a crowd. My own deep discomfort at being noticed by other people might help to explain my annoyance with someone like my loud coworker Ned. It could be that I grew up in a family where drawing attention to myself brought unwelcome consequences, so I learned to play it safe and keep quiet. By practicing acceptance and understanding toward someone else, especially when their behavior makes me uncomfortable, I am creating space to more fully see and accept myself.

Compassion and Purpose

The practice of Compassionate Seeing reminds us above all that our story is not *the* story. There is a greater reality, a larger picture of which we see only a very small part. In this way, Compassionate Seeing connects us to Purpose, the experience of belonging to something infinitely greater than ourselves. When we practice Compassionate Seeing, we recognize that our lives are intertwined with a story much bigger than our own. Uncovering this thread of connection between us is like plugging into a powerful current of abundant vitality and joy.

Judgments, on the other hand, disconnect us from Purpose by falsely suggesting that what we see is all there is. This makes it easy for us to blame others for what we perceive as their shortcomings or bad choices. Judgments sap our time, energy, and attention. They cause us to waste these invaluable commodities constructing false narratives. If we could see the whole picture—or the whole person—then other people's behavior would probably make far more sense to us than it does now. The more I know of someone else's story, the easier it is for me to accept that person for who they are, even if I find their actions difficult or troublesome. So if I am having a hard time practicing compassion toward someone else, I take that as a sign that I just don't know the whole story. I'm not seeing the big picture.

The Compassionate Universe

The universe favors compassion. This is the inescapable conclusion of the evolutionary process. Humans rose to prominence in the natural order by learning to perceive others as separate selves—people with their own thoughts, feelings, motivations, and desires— and then figuring out how to make an imaginative leap and see things from the others' perspective. We came to recognize that what is painful or unpleasant for us might be painful or unpleasant for others, too. This is the basis of communication and social cooperation, which have made possible all our advances in science and technology. Seen in this light, the Golden Rule is much more than a moral code. It is the secret of our success as a species. It is almost like a strand of the universe's DNA.

Compassion is literally woven into the fabric of the universe.

THE MANTRA
I Accept Everything I See

———————

At this point, I want to offer you a simple mantra that can help you practice Compassionate Seeing. A mantra is a powerful phrase you can repeat out loud or in your head as a way to focus your intentions. A mantra can be considered a kind of prayer, although this mantra will work even if you don't believe in a God. I like to think of the mantra as a bargain with the universe. I am committing to something, and the universe is going to do something in return. In my experience, the universe drives hard bargains, and sometimes I get more than I expect.

It's important to remember that the mantras recommended in this book are only tools, so if any of them doesn't work for you, just keep looking for something else that does.

The mantra for Compassionate Seeing is very simple: *I accept everything I see.* That's it. Don't judge it, don't avoid it, don't fight it or try to change it.

Unconditionally accept whatever presents itself. You can use the mantra at any time, but here are some times that I find especially good for saying this mantra:

- When looking at myself in the mirror, especially if I am feeling insecure about my appearance. *I accept everything I see.*

- When looking at my spouse, especially if we are having some kind of conflict. *I accept everything I see.*

- When looking at my children, especially when I am having a hard time recognizing the difference between myself and them. *I accept everything I see.*

- Anytime I notice someone's behavior is causing me discomfort or I start crafting a story in my head. *I accept everything I see.*

I invite you to try using this mantra several times a day for a week, repeating it silently in your mind or out loud to yourself. As you say the words, pay attention to what shows up. You are announcing your intention to accept whatever enters your field of awareness. Usually, we don't see things we are unwilling to accept, because the opposite of acceptance is denial. So when you start using the mantra, you may find yourself seeing things you hadn't noticed before. There are some things the universe simply will not show you until you are ready to accept them.

As you practice using this mantra, you may find

yourself resisting. I know I certainly did, and still do sometimes. You might hear a voice in your head objecting that you can't possibly accept everything, that some things are simply unacceptable. If this happens, I encourage you to become curious about this voice and query it gently: what bad thing might happen if you did accept everything that shows up in your life? Here are a few answers I came up with for myself:

- The job won't get done.

- The house will always be a mess.

- My needs in this relationship won't get met.

- People will walk all over me.

Whatever answers you come up with, I invite you to consider them. Remember, acceptance is not synonymous with approval. Accepting something doesn't mean I have to like it, nor does it mean I have to think it is good or right; in fact, "good" and "right" are just as much judgments as "bad" and "wrong."

Acceptance does not mean we cannot keep firm boundaries, or put appropriate safeguards in place, or maintain high standards. It doesn't mean we can't ask for what we want. But I find that when I'm not getting what I want in a relationship or a particular situation, practicing Compassionate Seeing and using the mantra can help me steer clear of my habitual storylines, familiar narratives that tell me I'm the victim or the good guy. Instead, I can ask questions like, "Why does this keep happening?" and "What does this look like from your perspective?" When I take this approach, I often start seeing new things that change my view of the person or situation.

Acceptance also does not mean that we will necessarily agree with everything other people say or do. In fact, disagreements are a healthy way of recognizing the difference between ourselves and others. If you and I don't see eye to eye on something, and I say to you, "We disagree," I am acknowledging that we have different points of view, different stories. When I am practicing Compassionate Seeing, this naturally leads me to engage in a discovery mindset and become curious about your point of view. I start to wonder about your perspective, and I want to learn more about how you see things.

But if I tell you you're wrong because your story doesn't line up with mine, this shuts down the conversation. I am failing to recognize the difference between me and you, and thereby missing the opportunity to see things from a new perspective. What I am really saying is that my point of view is binding on you, that my story trumps your story. I am treating you as an extension of myself, and not as a unique individual.

If you are someone who cares about social issues like poverty, discrimination, and injustice, you may wonder how Compassionate Seeing relates to matters like these. After all, if we accept everything, then how will anything ever change? This raises a very important question: what actually instigates change? In my experience, change most often occurs as a result of breaking through to a new way of seeing a problem. So the mindset that leads to change is necessarily flexible, open, and interested, not rigid or judgmental.

Judgments create a false sense of moral clarity, which leads to self-righteousness and self-justification. If I judge other people harshly for their unjust behavior, this will make it harder for me to see the ways I may be practicing injustice. When I accept something I don't like in someone else, on the other hand, I am learning to recognize and accept the same thing in myself. Change starts from within. So if we want to instigate change, it is absolutely imperative to practice Compassionate Seeing.

THE CHALLENGE
Compassion is Not a Feeling

———————

Compassionate Seeing is a practice, which means that, like any skill, we get better by doing it over and over again. There is no magic about it, no moment of illumination after which we will unfailingly see everyone and everything in the rosy glow of compassion. It will probably seem awkward and forced at first. Some days, I find the practice much easier than others. That's natural. The key is to practice as often as possible every day. I have discovered that the more I practice, the more energy and focus I have, because I'm no longer wasting mental resources trying to prove that I am right and someone else is wrong.

Some spiritual practices—including certain kinds of meditation or focused prayer—can engender warm and wonderful feelings of well-being and benevolence, the kinds of feelings we often associate with compassion.

On the surface, there is nothing wrong with this.

But feelings like these can also prompt us to avoid certain people, situations, or topics of conversation—anything we might find uncomfortable or upsetting. We might avoid difficult encounters in order to protect the glow of our benevolent feelings and preserve our sense of peace. The test of any practice is not the feelings it produces, but whether it helps us move into uncomfortable territory. Love is about going to uncomfortable places.

We must not mistake warm feelings for compassion. Compassion is not a feeling. It is a practice unto itself, a habit, a skill.

A simple parable may help illustrate this point.

A monk prayed fervently in the temple to experience compassion for all people. At the end of his prayer, he had a warm and wonderful feeling in his heart, and he knew his prayer had been answered. He happily departed the temple, but as he opened the door he bumped into another brother, who whirled around and gave him a shove. The first monk felt a hot flash of anger. He pushed the second monk back, and the two started shouting at each other and almost came to blows. Steaming with rage, the first monk stormed off to the kitchen to perform his daily duties. But nothing went right; everyone in the kitchen seemed especially irritable and the monk got into several arguments. In the confusion, supper got burned, and everyone blamed the first monk.

Finally, he could take no more. He rushed back to the temple and prayed again: "Lord, I thought you were going to put compassion for all people into my heart!" He heard a voice speaking from within, saying, "Yes, that is why I am putting all these people who need compassion in your way." The monk then understood that the answer to his prayers was not in the warm feeling, but in the daily encounters with all the flesh-and-blood people who crossed his path.

The universe drives hard bargains. Sometimes, when you ask for something, you may get more than you expect.

THE PRACTICE IN PRACTICE
I Wonder What It's Like to Be You

———————

You can practice Compassionate Seeing toward any-one—the embarrassed mother whose overtired child is having a fit in the grocery store, the well-dressed executive fidgeting impatiently at the back of the cof-fee shop line. Put yourself in the other person's place and ask, "I wonder what it's like to be you right now?" If someone is rude to you in the office or at the check-out counter, instead of reacting blindly in turn, try to become curious about what kind of day that person is having. If you are having an especially difficult time seeing someone else compassionately, visualize that person as a young child, perhaps two years old, and then ask, "I wonder what steps in your life's journey brought you here? What has happened to you along the way? What have others done to you, and what have you done to yourself?"

I find that my greatest allies in deepening my practice are those closest to me: my spouse, children, family, and friends. As I practice putting myself in their place and becoming curious about their experiences, I can also gain valuable feedback and refine my perceptions by asking them questions: "How did that make you feel? What were you hoping for in that conversation? What is it like living with me now?" When I ask these kinds of questions, I am often surprised by what I hear. I frequently discover things I didn't know about people I thought I knew very well. And this, in turn, serves to deepen my curiosity and opens my eyes to things I had previously overlooked.

Compassionate Seeing in Disagreement

Compassionate Seeing is particularly challenging in the midst of disagreement—when all you want is for the other person to see things your way, not the other way around.

Let's say a good friend of mine named Jim has decided to get a divorce. I feel certain he is making a big mistake. I like Jim's spouse, and our children go to school together. I hate to think of what will happen to their family if Jim pursues a divorce, and I don't think it's the best thing for him. I just can't bring myself to support his decision. I've tried to share my concerns many times, but Jim doesn't want to hear about it. The topic is starting to strain our relationship.

The best thing I can do is to put myself in Jim's place and try to understand where he's coming from—even if that doesn't change my opinion. This takes mental effort. It's not easy to walk in someone else's shoes. I can start by asking myself, "If I were the one in this situation, what would I be thinking and feeling? How would I want to be treated? What kind of friend would I want?" If the tables were turned, I probably wouldn't want someone to judge me or question my intentions as I was going through one of the most difficult decisions of my life. More likely, I would want someone who would simply show up, listen, and try to understand what I was going through.

It could be that Jim is feeling more deeply conflicted about leaving the marriage than he's letting on. He might be putting up a good front, knowing I am likely to seize on any sign of doubt as proof that the divorce is a mistake. By making a conscious effort to see compassionately, I can be the friend Jim really needs right now. He will be more likely to open up if he knows he can do so without fear of being judged.

Compassionate Seeing in the Workplace

People sometimes think of compassion as something that requires airbrushing over unpleasant truths and looking at the world through a fuzzy, slightly-out-of-focus lens. But the opposite is actually true. Compassionate Seeing allows us to view the world in sharp definition, without the distorted lenses of our judgments. Compassionate Seeing certainly isn't about being nice, if "nice" means never having hard conversations or holding others accountable for their behavior.

For this reason, Compassionate Seeing works just

as well in the workplace as it does in our other relationships. If you are a business owner, Compassionate Seeing can help you understand the needs of your customers and treat them the way you would want to be treated in their place. And Compassionate Seeing can help you become a better, more effective manager as well.

Let me give you an example of what Compassionate Seeing looks like in the workplace.

Say I am a manager, and I have an employee named Marsha who has performed well in the past but seems to have become very unmotivated lately. Marsha has been arriving late, leaving shifts early, and calling in sick—often on short notice. I call her into my office to find out what is going on. During the course of the conversation, I learn that Marsha's teenage son recently started hanging out with a tough crowd after school and getting into trouble. The teenager was arrested for shoplifting a few weeks ago, and Marsha had to leave work early to go to the police station. Since then, she's been trying to spend as much time at home with her son as possible, which explains the late arrivals and missed shifts.

In order to practice Compassionate Seeing in this situation, the first thing I have to do is to set aside my judgments. For instance, I might be tempted to assume Marsha has failed to provide her son with appropriate guidance and discipline, and is therefore a poor parent. That kind of thinking is probably just a way to make myself feel better about potentially having to fire someone in such a difficult situation. If I make an imaginative leap and put myself in her place, it will be plain to me that the problem isn't a lack of motivation or commitment, but a matter of conflicting priorities. This perspective helps me make sense of the situation and decide how to proceed.

I could then say something like this: "I can see that you're in a really difficult spot. I think if I were in your position I'd feel really scared about my child, so I can understand why you've been missing work lately. But we have a job to do here, and I need to let you know that you're on the verge of losing your position. How can we make this work?" I might be able to offer some time off or temporarily adjust her shifts so Marsha can spend more time at home after school.

Of course, if the situation doesn't improve, I may still have to let her go. Practicing Compassionate Seeing doesn't mean I will never fire or discipline anyone. But if I am able to salvage the situation, I will come away with a far more loyal and dedicated employee—someone who feels understood and appreciated and is highly motivated to contribute to the success of the company.

PART TWO
Heartfelt Listening

THE ISSUE
Deaf to Self

———

Once, there was an old woman who was reputed to be the wisest teacher in all the land. People even came from faraway countries to seek her counsel. There was always a crowd waiting outside her hut. People would go inside with their shoulders tight and hunched, and their eyes red from sleepless nights. But when they came out, their steps were lighter, and there was relief in their eyes. Everyone went away praising her profound insight and sage advice.

One day, a young seeker went to see the wise teacher and begged her to share the secret of her great wisdom. The teacher looked kindly at the seeker and said, "My child, when people come to see me, I welcome them and invite them to sit down. I know some people have come great distances carrying heavy burdens, so I try to make them as comfortable as I can. Then I ask them to tell me why they came, and I never interrupt while they answer. Even though I know others are waiting, I don't hurry people along or rush them to the point. I let them speak as long as they need. When they have said everything they have to say, I do not give them advice or try to solve their problems. I just say four simple words. Always the same four words, and no more."

The seeker begged the wise teacher to reveal the four magic words. The teacher leaned forward, and with a twinkle in her eye, she whispered, "Please tell me more."

Listening from the Heart

Listening is the most valuable gift you or I can give another person. This is what the teacher knew. She was wise enough not to try to solve other people's problems or answer all their questions. She understood that, usually, people have the solutions to their problems within themselves. Sometimes they just don't know it yet. If we listen to others long enough, they will find the answers to their own questions. All we have to do is keep repeating the four magic words: "Please tell me more."

Yet most of us are terrible listeners. Here's why: we are only as good at listening to others as we are at listening to our own heart.

Listening to your heart means paying attention to your feelings and what they are telling you. If I am uncomfortable with my own emotions, I will react to other people's emotions, and I won't be able to listen to them very well. For example, if someone starts expressing a strong feeling, such as anger or deep sadness, I might make a joke or try to change the subject. Or, I might start trying to solve that person's problem. Any of these responses reflect the reality that I'm uncomfortable with the other person's emotion. I do not want them to tell me more.

The Healing Power of Listening

Let me give you a practical example of how our inability to listen to ourselves leads to an inability to listen to others.

Let's say I have a sister who recently experienced a miscarriage. She is devastated by the loss of the pregnancy. I don't want her to feel so sad, so I keep my conversations with her positive and upbeat. I try to help her see the good in what has happened—after all, the pregnancy proves she is able to conceive, and she is still young enough to try again. I remind her that some people aren't able to get pregnant at all due to age or infertility, so she should be grateful that she was able get pregnant in the first place. I tell her that her baby is an angel in heaven now and wouldn't want her to be so sad.

As time goes on, my sister only seems to get sadder. I start noticing a tight, queasy feeling in my stomach whenever I talk to her. I avoid her calls because I just can't deal with hearing her cry on the other end of the phone all the time. I can't understand why she doesn't just get over it and move on. After all, that's what I did when my spouse and I went through a miscarriage a few years ago.

If I were to listen to my own heart in this situation, I'd see that I'm deeply uncomfortable with feelings of sadness and grief. I avoid these feelings in myself as much as possible, and when I encounter them in someone else, I suppress them or pivot away as quickly as I can. My sister's sadness is upsetting for me because it brings up old emotions I don't want to deal with. Before I can listen to her grief, I need to listen to mine.

THE FIX
Awakening to Joy

Heartfelt Listening means listening in such a way that our heart, our emotional center, is engaged and active in the hearing process. As we listen fully to others, we are also attuned to what our feelings and emotions are telling us. Here are the basic steps:

1. *Pay attention* to what is happening in your emotional world. Stay alert, and be attentive to whatever you feel. It may help to name your emotions as you notice them.

2. *Become aware of sensations* in your body, such as tightness in your shoulders, pain in your temples, or queasiness in your gut. These sensations can help clue you in to your emotional state.

3. *Recognize your reactions* to other people's emotions. Notice when you feel the need to solve someone's problems for them or when you dodge certain topics of conversation that are emotionally

charged. Don't judge these reactions, just recognize them.

4. *Welcome whatever you find* in your heart. Don't deny or compartmentalize your feelings, and don't try to suppress what other people are feeling, either. Remind yourself that whatever you feel is okay, and whatever others are feeling is okay, too.

The Two Vital Questions of Heartfelt Listening

The First Vital Question: What am I Feeling?
The practice of Heartfelt Listening is based on two vital questions. I consider these questions vital because they are life-giving—they have the power to restore vitality and joy.

The first vital question is, "What am I feeling?" Take a moment to ask yourself this question right now. Give what you are feeling a name: are you feeling happy, sad, angry, scared (these are the "primary colors" of the emotions), or something else? Be still and pay attention to whatever you feel. Become aware of and interested in your own emotions. Scan your body for sensations. Is your jaw clenched or relaxed? Is your breathing deep or restrained? Do you feel tension in your shoulders or your neck? Do you feel pain in your temples or your stomach? Are you sitting quietly or fidgeting? Your physical sensations are clues to your emotional state.

If you are having a hard time figuring out what

you're feeling, you might try asking a different question: "Is there anything I am trying not to feel?" Think back to the ways you've reacted to other people's emotions recently. Did anyone's anger, sadness, happiness, or fear make you feel uncomfortable? These reactions are clues as to what might be happening in your own inner world.

The Second Vital Question: What is This Feeling Telling Me?

The second vital question is, "What is this feeling telling me?" Think of your feelings as messages from your instinctive self, a part of us that is older and sometimes wiser than our rational self.

Feelings of grief and loss, for instance, are there to remind us of what is most precious in life—people and relationships, rather than money or things—so we can remember to pay attention to what really matters before it's too late. Fear, like pain, is unpleasant, but is there for a reason: to keep you safe. When you feel anxious or afraid, your heart is sending you a message: "I feel unsafe." Your rational self might be telling you that everything is fine, but if you have a gut instinct that something isn't quite right, you should try to understand what your heart is telling you. When you feel angry, your heart might be saying, "I want something to change"—even if change isn't a possibility your rational self is ready to consider.

Our heart is often a more reliable indicator of what we really want than our thoughts. If your rational self is telling you, "I want x," but your heart is saying, "No, not x. I want y!" that's a signal for you to start listening to your feelings in order to discover what is really going on.

DEEP DIVE
Acedia

The ancients speak of the heart as the well-spring of life, the source of life energy—what we might call "zest." This zest gives life flavor and richness. It is what makes life worth living.

Our emotions are all currents of this life energy. When these currents are flowing freely, we feel fully alive, and our body literally tingles with vitality. Being in touch with our feelings in this way makes it possible for us to connect with others at an emotional level. It is often through emotion and connection to others that we experience Purpose, belonging to that which is infinitely greater than ourselves. I have found that the more attuned I am to my heart, the more connected I feel to the universe and everything in it. This sense of deep connectedness can be a rich source of inner rejuvenation and refreshment.

But if our heart is blocked, if we deny our emotions or try to suppress them, life lacks zest and everything seems dull, empty, and meaningless. When people ignore what their heart is telling them for a long time, eventually they stop feeling anything at all. They don't feel angry or sad or scared any longer, but they don't feel any happiness or joy or connection to Purpose either. Their heart is blocked, and life has no zest. They just feel numb and burnt out.

The spiritual masters of the Egyptian desert have a technical term for this condition. They call it *acedia* (pronounced *ah-key-THEE-ah*), which comes from a Greek word meaning "inattentiveness" or "neglect." *Acedia* signifies a failure to attend to something that needs nurturing, like a garden that needs watering and cultivation. It is used to describe a state of torpor, listlessness, or despair that results from not paying attention to the heart. *Acedia* is not the same as depression, although it can lead to depression. *Acedia* is numbness, a state of unfeeling, disconnection from our deepest self.

Sometimes, *acedia* can manifest as malaise, a bad mood we just can't shake. I may notice that I feel constantly cranky and irritable and don't know why, or I may feel down all the time for no apparent reason. In other cases, people may experience this numbness because they fill their time with frenetic activity and endless distractions. They never slow down long enough to listen to what their heart is saying.

Acedia is dangerous. Not only does it sap our energy and motivation for working hard and engaging with others, but it can lead some people to self-medicate with drugs, pornography, or meaning-less sexual encounters. People may slip into these destructive behaviors because they are just trying to feel alive again. When I experience any symptom of *acedia*, I take it as a cue that I need to start paying more attention to what's happening in my heart.

The Basis for Empathy

Compassionate Seeing and Heartfelt Listening sup-port and build on one another. When practiced together, they form the basis for empathy, which is the capacity to be moved by others' emotions. It is the highest form of understanding, because we are connected to the other person not only through the mind, but also the heart.

Empathy for another person begins with Compassionate Seeing: I make an imaginative leap and try to put myself in that person's place. As I imag-ine what it would be like to be in their position, I also become curious about their emotions. I start to won-der, "If I were the one in this situation, what would I be feeling?" The deeper I go in this creative exploration of the other's experience, the more I may notice that I am feeling sad about what makes them sad, happy for what makes them happy, or angry over what makes them angry. I am moved by what moves them. I can then reflect back what I am feeling in response: "I am so sad about what happened," or "It really makes me mad to hear how you were treated," or "I'm so happy that you accomplished your goal!" When we engage with others at an emotional level, they feel more deeply heard and understood by us.

Empathy comes naturally if I've cultivated acceptance through Compassionate Seeing and emotional awareness through Heartfelt Listening—and it's impossible if I'm living in a state of *acedia*.

THE MANTRA
I Hear What My Heart is Saying

———————

The mantra for Heartfelt Listening helps us focus our attention on what's happening in our emotional realm. The mantra goes like this: *I hear what my heart is saying.* Like the first mantra, you can use the second mantra at any time throughout the day, and you can drop it if it doesn't work for you. Here are some times that I find this mantra especially useful:

- When I feel happy, cheerful, or content. *I hear what my heart is saying.*

- When I am experiencing a strong emotion, like anger, fear, or sadness. *I hear what my heart is saying.*

- When I feel numb and life lacks zest. *I hear what my heart is saying.*

- When other people's emotions make me feel uncomfortable or reactive. *I hear what my heart is saying.*

I recommend saying this mantra out loud or in your head a few times every day for the next week. Remember, using a mantra means striking a deal with the universe. By saying this mantra, you are committing to listen to whatever your heart is telling you—and you should be prepared to hear some surprising things. When the universe is trying to send you a message, that message most often comes to you by way of your heart, not through your thoughts.

Be prepared for this to be deeply uncomfortable. When we first start listening to our heart after not doing so for a while, it's a little like getting the blood flowing again to a foot that has gone to sleep. The sensations can be painful.

You might discover an emotion you didn't know you had—and it might feel threatening. I sometimes find that my heart has been telling me things for a long time that I have been trying to ignore. Once I recognize an emotion for the first time, I can't pretend it isn't there. I have to figure out what to do about it. That's part of the bargain. You also might experience a strong emotion that makes you feel like you're not in control, and most of us resist losing control more than just about anything.

Sometimes, my rational self comes up with all kinds of reasons why listening to my emotions is dangerous. Here's a short list of excuses I have used in the past for not listening to my heart:

- I would have to admit that I'm not happy in this relationship.

- I might just decide to quit this job.

- I would speak my mind more often, and that could get me into trouble.

- I'm afraid the grief would never end.

You have your own list of reasons. Whatever is on it, I encourage you to sit with it and try to understand where the resistance is coming from. Our rational self often tries to protect us from painful feelings and experiences. But at what cost? Not listening to our heart may keep us from pain, but it also holds us back from all kinds of experiences that lead to personal growth and happiness. I have discovered that I have much more happiness in my life when I pay attention to what my heart is saying, even if the message seems scary or painful at first.

The way to be happy is to listen to your heart.

THE CHALLENGE
Chasing Peace and Joy

We all crave peace and joy. Yet, so few of us truly know what it means to experience either. We consider joy the opposite of sadness, anger, and fear. We believe peace exists only in their absence.

In our culture, these assumptions are unsurprising. But that doesn't make them correct.

Think back to a time when you really got in touch with some strong emotion. Maybe you were able to release some anger that had been building up for a while, to get mad and stomp and shout. Or you were able to weep for some deep sadness or loss, to heave and rock as the tears streamed down your face. After either of these experiences, you probably felt more fully alive than you did beforehand.

This experience of feeling fully alive is what joy is all about. Joy is not the opposite of anger or fear or sadness. Joy is the experience of being fully in touch with our emotions, feeling emotional currents as life energy coursing through our body. I often find that joy is underneath the emotion I am trying to avoid. I have to go through one to get to the other.

When we make a habit of paying attention to what we feel and listening to what these feelings are telling us, eventually we arrive at the place of full emotional integration. We know that whatever we feel is okay, and whatever others feel is okay, too.

The best word for this state of being is peace. This is an often-misunderstood and misused word in the spiritual life. Peace is not the absence of strong emotions like anger, grief, or fear. Peace means looking deep into our heart and welcoming whatever we find there. When I am at peace, I'm not fighting my emotions or trying to suppress them, nor am I clinging to them, trying to hold on to certain feelings or preserve a particular emotional state. I become aware of my feelings as they arise, peak, and subside. I recognize my emotions for what they are: surges of energy, like waves breaking on a beach. They roll in, they crest, and they recede again.

Misguided Spirituality

Some spiritual teachers tell their followers they should experience less and less strong emotions like anger, fear, sadness, or lust—which they sometimes call "negative" emotions—as they progress along the spiritual path. They may even claim that, as advanced spiritual practitioners, they have reached the stage where they are no longer troubled by such feelings, but abide in a state of constant and undisturbed peace and joy.

I find this kind of teaching unhelpful, and even dangerous. It is unhelpful because it creates an expectation that truly "spiritual" people do not have certain kinds of feelings. So, according to this logic, I have to make sure never to experience such emotions if I want to be spiritual. As a result, I will shy away from people and places that bring up strong emotions, cutting myself off from valuable relationships. I will avoid hard conversations or conflict with others, shunning situations that require uncomfortable honesty.

Following such teachings can eventually lead to *acedia*, emotional numbness and disconnection. I might even mistake *acedia* for spiritual progress. But the spiritual life is not about avoiding emotions or transcending them, it is about experiencing life to the full. Emotions are part of this. Even "negative" emotions like fear, anger and grief have a positive purpose. They are there to keep us safe, to let us know when change is needed, and to remind us of what is most precious in life.

Sexual Energy

Sexual feelings often get thrown in the "negative" category. As children, many of us were taught to attach guilt or shame to these feelings. But, like other emotions, sexual energy also belongs to the heart, and it's important to listen to our sexual feelings and understand what they are telling us.

Say I am in a committed relationship, but I have started having sexual feelings for someone other than my partner. As time goes on, these feelings continue to get stronger and stronger. My inclination may be to ignore these feelings or deny them because I don't want to be unfaithful. I also don't want conflict with my partner. I just want joy and peace. But for the sake of my relationship, it's better to listen to what these feelings are telling me rather than block them out. This doesn't mean I act on those feelings—it just means I acknowledge their presence and query their meaning.

If I listen closely, I may hear my heart saying something like this: "I'm bored in this relationship. I want to feel excited and alive, and I don't feel that way right now. I want to fall in love again."

As difficult as it may be, it's time to start communicating with my partner about how I'm feeling. This could be an opportunity to renew our relationship and rekindle our love for each other. But if I ignore what my heart is telling me, the problem may only get worse. My relationship will lack zest, and eventually I might even have an affair in an attempt to feel alive again. By listening to my heart, even if the message is uncomfortable, I stay in touch with my life energy, and this can bring new vitality to my relationship with my partner.

THE PRACTICE IN PRACTICE
Please Tell Me More

Just like Compassionate Seeing, Heartfelt Listening is often difficult for parents. I find that I often react strongly to my children's emotions, and it took a while for me to learn that this is worth paying attention to.

Our reactions to our children's feelings often reflect how our parents responded to our emotions when we were children. For many of us, childhood was the time when we first started learning how to ignore our heart. Parents sometimes unconsciously send the message that their children's feelings are not acceptable. We tell our children, "Don't cry," or "Don't be scared." Occasionally, these messages can be gender-specific: boys don't cry, and girls don't yell. When parents do this, it doesn't mean they are bad or uncaring people. Usually, they are doing the very best they can, and they are likely passing along messages they internalized from their own parents. We can disrupt these kinds of generational cycles by consciously and consistently sending the message to our children that whatever they feel is okay. But to do this, we have to be willing to listen to our own feelings.

Say, for instance, I have a young son who is playing on a softball team, but is afraid of being hit by the ball. Every time the ball comes anywhere near him, my little ballplayer flinches and turns away. I notice that I cringe and my gut clenches whenever this happens. As the innings go on, I start to feel very self-conscious, like all the other parents are glaring at me because my child is costing our team the game. The next time it happens, I start yelling in an exasperated tone, "C'mon, don't be so ball-shy! Catch it! Run after it!" Our team ends up losing the game. As we drive home in the car afterward, I am preoccupied with my own thoughts. I realize that the sensations I had at the ballpark are the same feelings I used to have when I played sports as a child. I remember one of my parents standing on the sidelines and yelling at me whenever I missed the ball or made a mistake. I remember the silence in the car on the way home when my team lost a game. I remember feeling ashamed.

When we get home from the game, I realize that I have been quiet in the car the whole way, and so has my son. After dinner, I decide to initiate a conversation about what happened. We sit down on the couch together, and I ask, "What does it feel like when the ball is coming at you really fast?" Because I am paying attention to my own feelings and have some understanding of where they come from, I am able to listen to my child's feelings without reacting to them. I'm comfortable asking him to tell me more.

In response, I offer reassurance that there is nothing wrong with feeling afraid. I tell him stories of times when I felt scared and talk about how I found the courage to go forward. Courage, after all, doesn't mean denying or suppressing fear. It means acknowledging our fear and then facing it. By talking openly about my own fears and how I faced them, I am modeling healthy emotional awareness for my son and starting a new generational cycle of Heartfelt Listening.

Heartfelt Listening in the Workplace

There is often an implicit assumption that emotions have no place in a professional workplace setting. But we are emotional beings, and we cannot simply check our feelings at the door. Nor should we. Our emotions lend passion, vitality, and zest to our work, making Heartfelt Listening a useful skill in the workplace.

Let's say I am in a meeting discussing an important project. The project hasn't been going well, and my co-workers and I are trying to figure out what's going wrong. Everyone is on edge because a report to management on the status of the project is due later that week. The atmosphere in the room is tense, and people are starting to snipe at each other. Unexpectedly, a colleague named Tim says something that suggests I haven't been doing my job, and that this is why the project is not on track.

I feel an immediate flush of anger—my cheeks get hot, my breathing gets shallow, my muscles tense, my pulse quickens. My whole body tingles with a rush of energy. One option is to suppress my anger. I could pretend I didn't hear what was said, or ignore it. Even though my body is trembling, I could act as if everything is fine. I could maintain control and not lose my cool. Another response would be to react and direct my anger at Tim. I could go on the attack, raising my voice, insisting he is wrong, questioning his motivations, maybe even making some accusations of my own in the process.

There is yet another way to respond that doesn't involve suppressing my anger or directing it outward. The first step is to focus on my feelings, to become aware of the physical sensations of anger. I let myself feel my face getting hot, my pulse rising, my breathing getting shallow, and I acknowledge to myself, "I'm feeling really mad about this." I experience anger for what it is: a surge of energy in my body.

Next, though my voice may shake a little, I acknowledge my feeling out loud with as much calm as I can muster: "I'm feeling pretty angry right now because I think you're questioning my competence or my integrity, or maybe both. I need a moment to cool off, but then I'd like you to tell me more about what you're thinking. I want to understand what you think my role is in the problems we've been having and what you suggest we do about it."

I leave the room for a minute to get a drink of water and take a couple of deep breaths. The physical manifestations of anger start to fade. When I come back into the room, everything has changed. Tim apologizes for the remark. Everyone acknowledges that blaming each other is not going to help solve the problem. People are starting to think more creatively about the project, and some new ideas are starting to emerge. There is a new energy in the room. Just acknowledging the emotional current in the air made the tension dissipate. This is how much influence one person can have when they listen to their heart.

PART THREE
Intentional Welcoming

THE ISSUE
Too Much Yes

One night, three robbers broke into the hut of a monk who lived alone in the desert. When the monk realized what was happening, he remained seemingly unfazed. He simply nodded to greet his uninvited guests, then returned to braiding ropes out of palm fibers by lamplight. Two of the robbers kept a nervous eye on the monk while the third began rifling through his possessions. There wasn't much of value in the hut, but the third robber loaded a handful of tools and several books into his pack. Still, the monk did not protest.

Then the robber picked up the robe the monk wore to the temple, noticing its fine, silken weave. At this, the owner of the hut looked up and said, calmly, "You cannot have that." The robber ignored the monk, shoved the robe into his pack, and headed for the door. But the monk stood up and said again, a little louder, "You cannot have that." The robbers were alarmed. They could see now that the monk was a very large man. The two who were standing guard grabbed his arms to restrain him, but the monk, who had spent his lifetime doing hard manual labor, shook them off almost effortlessly. He took a step toward the third robber and repeated once more, "You cannot have that."

Terrified, the third robber dropped his pack and ran, the other two scrambling over one another to get out of the door behind him. The monk followed them outside and called, "Wait!" In their confusion, the robbers stopped. The monk stepped back into the hut, and reemerged a moment later with the pack. He'd removed the robe, but the other items remained. "You forgot something," he said.

We Don't Mean Yes

How good are you at saying no? The monk in the story knew his limits and was not afraid to state them clearly, even in a tense and unpredictable situation.

Often, however, I find it hard to do the same. Many of us have trouble setting clear boundaries, especially with friends and family members, because we want to be liked and don't want to start conflict or disappoint anyone. We say yes because it's easy—not because it's really what we mean. Often, we believe saying yes is essential to being a good employee, a good daughter or son, a good member of our religious community, a nice person. Saying no feels stingy or rude—yet saying yes when we don't mean it damages our relationships.

Let's say, for example, that I have a coworker who sometimes asks to borrow money for lunch. We work for a large company with its own cafeteria where everyone on our team buys their midday meal. My colleague always promises to pay me back after the next paycheck, but typically doesn't follow through. I haven't brought it up, because I'm trying to be nice. I like to think of myself as a generous person. With time, the requests become more frequent—all the way up to once a week, and I'm feeling exasperated.

If I can't figure out how to establish my limits, resentment and anger will inevitably build up, potentially ruining my relationship with this person. I might avoid him or act distant when we interact, hoping he gets the hint. Eventually, I might even abandon socializing with my team in the cafeteria and opt for eating lunch at my desk instead, allowing this one awkward situation to inhibit my relationships with a dozen other people. Inaction in this situation clearly doesn't lead to positive results—and we all know that losing my temper with this person isn't going to preserve the relationship or benefit my reputation in the office.

My best alternative is to honestly establish boundaries with this coworker. I might say, "I can't keep loaning money to you because it's negatively affecting our friendship. I'm trying to get better at establishing healthy boundaries." If he responds respectfully, I might even pursue a conversation about the financial difficulties he seems to be having. Maybe my colleague would prefer to bring his lunch from home in order to save money, but isn't doing so because he's afraid of standing out. If I knew this, I could offer to bring my lunch from home, too, so we could both save money without feeling like outsiders at the lunch table.

Saying yes when we don't mean it leads to a life of exhaustion and resentment. We burn out because we've agreed to too many commitments. We begrudge the friend or family member who consistently takes advantage of our generosity. We wonder why we simultaneously crave retreat from our community and deeper connection to it.

At the heart of this problem is a clear lack of intentionality. We have not identified specific priorities. We have not drawn clear boundaries to protect those priorities. We do not say yes and no with purpose, which leaves us taxingly disconnected from Purpose.

THE FIX

Saying No for the Greater Good

Intentional Welcoming is the ability to say no and mean it so we can say yes to the things that matter most. Setting limits and saying no are essential aspects of this spiritual practice. Here are some simple steps to help you establish and defend healthy boundaries:

1. *Make conscious decisions* about what you prioritize. Ask yourself the question, "What is really most important to me?" You can't do everything or please everyone. Make deliberate choices about what comes first in your life instead of letting others choose for you by default.

2. *Clearly define your limits*. Create some simple rules to safeguard these choices. For example, you might say, "I will leave work promptly at 5:15 p.m. every day so I can eat dinner with my family." By setting this limit on your work time, you conserve precious resources—your time and your

energy—so they can be devoted to the best possible use.

3. *Politely but firmly decline* every request and invitation that does not align with the priorities you have set. Don't waver, even if you sense that other people are disappointed or displeased. Respect your own limits, and others will learn to respect them as well.

4. *Warmly and graciously welcome* people and opportunities into your life in alignment with your highest values. By saying no to lesser things, you open up space in your life to spend precious resources on what matters.

The Two Steps of Intentional Welcoming

The First Step: Making Invitations
When we want to start practicing Intentional Welcoming, we must begin by clearly defining our priorities. In order to become more intentional about what we are welcoming into our life, we first need to clarify what really matters to us. Here's a simple exercise that I use to help me focus on what is most important.

Set aside a few minutes, get a pen and paper, and write down this question: "What would I do right now if I had more time, energy, and money?" Then, start writing whatever comes to mind. Anything is game. Don't rule something out just because it seems too big or impractical, or because you aren't sure it will make the final cut. Here are a few examples of things I have put down in the past:

- I would have more fun with my children and spouse.

- I would spend more time on creative activities like painting or writing.

- I would travel overseas.

- I would exercise more regularly.

- I would start taking steps on my business venture.

When the flow of ideas slows down, reconsider each item on the list and narrow it down to the options that make you feel the most excited and inspired—not the options that are the most doable. Two or three is plenty, and more than five is too many. The shorter the list, the more effective it will be.

If you have trouble coming up with things to write down, here's a simple rule of thumb: *follow the energy*. Don't add anything to the list out of a sense of duty, guilt, or obligation. Instead, focus on what brings you energy, vitality, and joy. As I consider whether to put something on my list, I practice Heartfelt Listening and ask myself, "How do I feel about this possibility? Does my heart say yes to this?" Energy and zest are the heart's way of saying yes to things. Sometimes, we might even feel our pulse quicken when our heart says yes. If you feel energized about something, write it down, even if that energy feels a little bit like fear.

I think of this as an *invitation list*. The items on

the list are all things I want to say yes to more often. I put the list in a place where I can see it every day. From time to time, I take a moment to repeat what is on the list silently to myself, changing the words "I would" to "I will," as in, "*I will* have more fun with my family." When we focus attention on our priorities in this way, opportunities naturally begin to flow in our direction. I may start to notice a lot of fun new activities I can do with my family. Connections, potential partners, even funding opportunities may show up for my business venture. New possibilities will begin to reveal themselves. The universe responds to invitations. Pay careful attention so you don't miss these replies.

The Second Step: Setting Limits

The second phase of Intentional Welcoming is saying no and setting limits. Oftentimes, people want to stop at the first step. They try to add new activities to their already full schedules, but they aren't able to sustain them. One of the reasons we often fail to follow through on our New Year's resolutions is that we try to say yes to new commitments without also carving out space for them. Like a juggler who keeps adding more and more balls, we falsely think our "new and improved" self will be efficient enough to keep doing everything we were already doing, plus take on major new endeavors.

Don't believe it. We can't say yes to everything, and if we try, we become so saturated with trivial commitments that we end up having to pass on more important opportunities when they arise. I have discovered that if I want to open up to new possibilities, I have to learn how to say no and set limits on other, less meaningful pursuits.

This second step, then, is pruning for the sake of Purpose. Think of your "no" as a sharp tool for cutting dead wood out of your life so the green branches can flourish. Any time you are making decisions about how to spend your time and resources, ask yourself, "Does this align with my priorities? Does it give me energy? Is my heart in it?" If not, say no to it. Be fierce. Whatever you do, do it because you want to or don't do it at all. I find that I have far more vitality and zest in my life if I relentlessly eliminate whatever I am currently doing half-heartedly and instead focus only on what brings positive energy, enthusiasm, and joy. Instead of feeling depleted at the end of each task, I am energized and ready to keep going.

If I have even a doubt or a question in my mind about whether to say yes to something, I find that it's better to say no. There's a very practical reason for this: it is always easier to say yes after we have said no than to say no once we have said yes. You can always go back and say yes later, but saying no later means going back on your word. I sometimes worry that if I say no, other people will be disappointed or angry with me, and I might lose my relationship with them. But most of the time, people respectfully accept the decisions of those who honor their own boundaries and priorities enough to be honest and decline.

We're Not Too Busy

I can't tell you how frequently I hear people around me say, "Sorry, I'm too busy." I used to say it, too, and these days busyness is often perceived as a status symbol. We one-up each other over how many hours we work or how many commitments we squeeze into the weekends.

Don't fall into this trap.

If an opportunity is life-giving, carve out time in your schedule for it. If it's not, decline with honesty. When I am practicing Intentional Welcoming, I don't feel the need to say, "I'm too busy." Instead, I make conscious decisions about whether I want to invite the opportunity that is being presented into my life. If not, I say, "That isn't something I can prioritize right now." Or, I just say, "No thank you."

DEEP DIVE
Sacred Boundaries

———————

Oftentimes, we use the word "boundary" solely to describe keeping someone out—limiting the time a former spouse can spend with our child, cutting off a flow of financial support to a struggling sibling, dialing back the frequency with which our in-laws show up unannounced.

But boundaries are not just against. They are *for*—and learning to articulate what our boundaries are for is an essential part of Intentional Welcoming.

A boundary exists to safeguard something special, a precious resource set apart for a particular purpose. For example, our government sometimes sets aside land to create a sanctuary for birds or other wildlife. The authorities clearly mark the boundary, and they do not allow cattle or motorized vehicles to cross into the refuge and destroy the habitat. The boundary does not exist solely for the purpose of keeping vehicles and grazing animals out, but for protecting and preserving what lives within.

Likewise, when we practice Intentional Welcoming, we are creating a sanctuary, a protected area in our life. We set up boundaries to preserve our health, time, energy, and money. We don't do this so we can keep them for ourselves alone, but so that we can share them with others without becoming physically and emotionally depleted. Rather than diffusing these resources amongst many competing demands, we focus them where they can accomplish the most good. We say no to some requests and opportunities so we can warmly and intentionally say yes to others and give them our full energy and attention.

Setting a boundary is a sacred act. The word "sacred" comes from the Latin *sacer*, which means something set apart or devoted to a particular use. Every holy place—every sacred precinct, temple, or shrine—is defined by its boundaries. Likewise, when we fix boundaries for ourselves, we are demarcating a zone that is set apart. We mark out certain times and activities as sacred, and we keep them inviolate. This could be time spent with a friend, attending your child's music recitals, or volunteering for a cause you believe in. It could mean choosing not to read social media postings during the workday so you can focus on your tasks, or not looking at work-related messages in the evening so you can give your full attention to your family. Whatever it is, you are cordoning off space in your life and holding it sacred.

Boundaries and Fierceness

Protecting and preserving this sacred space requires fierceness. We have be vigilant in holding our boundaries. Fierceness is anger channeled into a particular purpose. Remember, anger is just life energy, and fierceness simply means taking that energy and using it to create and maintain a boundary. Only if you are in touch with your anger can you manifest fierceness. This is one way that Intentional Welcoming builds on Heartfelt Listening.

You will always encounter resistance when you establish a new boundary. Count on it. You should expect pushback, and it could very well come from those closest to you. Rather than taking this personally, think of it as the universe testing your resolve. It's an opportunity to demonstrate the seriousness of your commitment. If you honor your own boundaries, others will learn to respect them as well.

THE MANTRA
I Honor the Boundaries I Set

Mustering the fierceness required to maintain our boundaries isn't always easy—especially in the midst of uncomfortable pushback. I've found that the simple mantra *I honor the boundaries I set* helps me focus my energy and remember why I set boundaries in the first place. My boundaries honor sacred spaces in my life, and they help me honor my community by offering my most genuine, enthusiastic self. I recommend saying this mantra several times a day during the next week to help you honor the commitments you've made. Here are some situations where I find it especially helpful:

- When I am engaged in an activity that is positive and life-giving, and I realize I want more of this kind of energy in my life. *I honor the boundaries I set.*

- When I want to say no to something, but I am

feeling pressure or obligation to give in and say yes. *I honor the boundaries I set.*

- When I feel unsure whether I should agree to do something I am being asked to do. *I honor the boundaries I set.*

- When I feel harried or overwhelmed by too many conflicting priorities. *I honor the boundaries I set.*

Like the first two mantras, the third mantra represents yet another bargain with the universe. We are promising to honor our boundaries by holding them firmly and using our resources well. That's our end of the bargain. And in return, we can be absolutely sure that the universe is going to test these boundaries. You may get comments suggesting that you have changed, or even that you aren't as nice as you used to be. When someone says something like this to me, I say the mantra silently in my head and try to take what was said as a compliment. It's true: I *am* changing. The spiritual life isn't about being nice, if "nice" means always doing what other people want and not honoring my own priorities. We shouldn't take this kind of talk personally. Instead, we can think of such encounters as the universe probing our resolve.

As we demonstrate that our boundaries are strong and we have enough self-respect to firmly maintain them, the universe will start sending us opportunities worthy of our time and attention, things we will want to say yes to. That's also part of the bargain. Instead of whiling the hours away on frivolous pursuits that bring no satisfaction, we will spend more and more of our time engaged in activities that are truly meaningful and worthwhile. Rather than feeling tired and drained all the time, we will feel energized and fully alive because we are living life on our own terms.

THE CHALLENGE
Dance of Differentiation

Some spiritual teachers say holding boundaries is a task for the spiritually immature, whereas advanced spiritual practitioners have no further need for boundaries because they are one with everything. According to this teaching, the goal of the spiritual life is to dissolve the boundaried self (sometimes referred to as the ego) so as to experience the limitless self.

As attractive as this teaching might sound, however, it does not reflect how the universe actually works, and it can lead to some very undesirable outcomes. Every living being has boundaries. Cells have walls that allow nutrients to pass through while keeping out toxins and invaders. Trees have bark to keep out insects and pests and to protect against fire. Our bodies have layers of skin to protect us from infection and disease. Boundaries are necessary for good health.

The goal of spiritual development is that each of

us should grow into a unique individual with boundaries that are both firm and flexible, so we can connect with others and maintain healthy separation at the same time. Without a firm sense of our boundaries, we are apt to become enmeshed in unhealthy emotional attachments, merging with others until we have no sense of our own identity. But if our boundaries become too rigid and inflexible, we cut ourselves off from life giving interactions and stop the flow of positive energy into our life.

One of the spiritual masters of the Egyptian desert beautifully captured the tension with this saying about some brothers who were not maintaining proper limits with each other: "Their barn door is always open, and anyone who wishes can come in and loose the donkey." Think of your boundaries as doors you can open or close whenever you need to. If the door is always open, you will constantly be invaded, watching helplessly as your "donkey"—your resources and life energy—are carried away without your consent. But if the door is always closed, nothing can get in or out, and your life will be empty and devoid of meaning. It will just be you and the donkey. Thriving happens in the tension between firm and flexible, open and closed.

Differentiation and Attachment

The universe expresses oneness through dynamic interconnection and interdependence. Millions of cells connect to create one living organism. Thousands of different species constitute one interdependent ecosystem.

Every organism, in order to survive and thrive, needs two conditions: attachment and differentiation. Too much attachment without differentiation, and the organism is engulfed, deteriorates, and dissolves. But too much differentiation without attachment, and the organism withers off and dies, disconnected from the source of life.

The universe is a dance of differentiation and attachment, autonomy and interdependence. From the moment we came into being, we have lived in the tension between these poles. We are different. We are one. Healthy attachment and differentiation enable us to remain connected to the source, to Purpose, so that life energy and love can flow through us. We need limits that are firm but also flexible to maintain this bond. If we harden our boundaries to the point of isolation, or weaken them to the point of dissolution, we lose the connection. The point is to stay connected, to join in the dance.

As we learn to negotiate our relationships skillfully, we become like expert dancers gliding in unison across the floor, maintaining contact through their fingertips, the energy flowing from one to the other like an electric current. Now closer, now farther apart, now approaching, now receding, we maintain the dynamic tension of connectedness.

THE PRACTICE IN PRACTICE
The Toughest Boundaries

———

Holding boundaries is always difficult, but especially when we have to set limits with people we care about deeply.

For example, it's often tough for adult children to negotiate new terms in their relationship with their parents. Without meaning to, parents sometimes resist their children's efforts to set healthy limits for themselves. They may say things that create feelings of guilt or shame, like "Don't let your spouse boss you around like that," or "You're making me sick worrying about you," or "You never call me." Parents who make these kinds of remarks might feel afraid of losing their connection to their children. But this kind of pressure can easily backfire, provoking resistance and emotional distancing. Relationships can only flourish in an atmosphere of mutual respect and trust. Boundaries are essential to creating and sustaining this kind of environment. It may seem counterintuitive, but holding firm limits prevents guilt and resentment from building up, and can actually strengthen bonds of healthy connection and attachment between adult children and their parents.

It can also be excruciatingly difficult for parents to do the opposite—to hold firm boundaries with their adult children, especially if the children are in some kind of trouble or are having a hard time establishing financial independence. Parents have a natural tendency to want to rescue their children from physical and emotional distress. But if they do this repeatedly, they may become so exhausted and the relationship so strained that the thread of their connection eventually snaps. In a situation like this, setting clear limits can be a way of conserving physical and emotional resources in order to sustain the relationship in the long term.

Say, for instance, I have an adult child, my youngest, who has become addicted to drugs. He has been in and out of rehab several times and has experienced homelessness on a few occasions, sleeping in a car or at a local shelter. My child frequently calls me in desperation, asking for money to buy food or prevent an eviction, or else wanting to stay with me in my home. At other times, I might go for months without hearing anything from him, and his cell phone is frequently disconnected for long stretches. I feel tortured by guilt, wondering where I went wrong. I feel like a failure as a parent.

Instead of blaming either my child or myself,

I could start by practicing Compassionate Seeing. Making a conscious effort to view the situation without judgment will help me recognize that parents are not responsible for the choices of their adult children, and people who are addicted are not intentionally hurting those they love. I could also practice Heartfelt Listening and acknowledge the incredible pain, sadness, and fear I am feeling. Though it's hard for me to admit, I'm also feeling really angry. By listening to my heart, I will know at a deep level that whatever I feel is okay, while also acknowledging that I cannot make these feelings go away by trying to fix my child's problems.

These exercises prepare me for setting a boundary with my positive intentions in mind. I want to be available to help and support my youngest through the long and arduous process of recovery. I want to be there for the long haul. This means that whatever approach I take must be sustainable over time. If I wear myself down by repeatedly intervening, loaning money and allowing my child to stay with me, I may reach the point where I become so exhausted and drained by the situation that I can no longer sustain our connection. My son may not like it, but by setting healthy limits I am preserving my physical, emotional, and financial well-being so I can continue to be present and available in our relationship.

In this situation, I would be wise to set specific limits around what kind of help I will and will not give moving forward. I might decide not to allow my son to stay at my house because he has a record of stealing from me when he sleeps over. At the same time, I could make clear that I want to maintain connection with him by suggesting that we meet regularly at a local restaurant or coffee shop. I might also decide not to give him money, but instead agree to purchase groceries or other necessities once a month so I know he's taken care of without having to worry the money is going to ill use.

Holding these boundaries can help prevent resentment and frustration from building up, because I am acting on my own terms rather than feeling manipulated. Practicing Intentional Welcoming in this situation makes it possible for me to protect my own well-being while sustaining my commitment to my child's welfare and recovery. Although there are no guarantees, this maximizes the chance that our relationship will be strong when my youngest is ready to make a change, and that I will have the strength I need to accompany him along the long path of recovery from addiction.

Boundaries in the Workplace

Our culture strongly pushes back against the idea of setting boundaries at work. Businesses reward employees who stay late and work from home in the evenings and on weekends. We're told the way to success is to say yes to everything, even if it means overtaxing ourselves. But establishing healthy boundaries in the workplace doesn't have to mean sacrificing career advancement. Intentional Welcoming can actually increase productivity and, with time, change entire teams for the better.

Let's say I work for a company where most of my colleagues work late—sometimes so late they order dinner delivery—and often go out for drinks together when they finally leave the office. The workload is heavy, and people frequently come in on weekends or take work home with them in order to meet deadlines.

Despite this, I decide I want to volunteer as a coach on my child's soccer team. This is not only an opportunity for me to spend more time with my own child, but also a chance to have a positive impact in the lives of other young people. I have great memories of sports coaches from my own childhood. They became trusted mentors and had a profound influence in my life outside of sports. I want to be able to have that kind of relationship with other kids, to make a real difference at a critical time in their development.

In order for me to serve as a coach, I will need to leave the office right at 5:00 p.m. most weekdays to make it on time for evening practices, and I will also have to keep my weekends open for scrimmages and games. When the soccer season starts, I begin implementing my new schedule, turning off my computer and leaving promptly at the end of the work day. After a couple of days of this new routine, I begin to hear comments from my coworkers suggesting they no longer see me as a team player. When I have to explain to my manager that I'm not available to work on a weekend, my boss is clearly not pleased. I'm starting to feel nervous and tense at the end of each day, as if all eyes are on me when I pack up and leave while others are still working.

In order to maintain my boundary, I need to summon some fierceness. It's important for me to clearly articulate my positive intention in setting these limits—and to do so in a way that isn't defensive, but is firm and respectful of my boundaries. I could say to my manager, "I've recently started volunteering as a coach on my child's soccer team. This is an important priority for me, and it means I've had to set some new limits in terms of my schedule. I want you to know that I'm still committed to the success of our team. I'll come in early if I have to, and I'll continue to make sure my work gets done on time. I appreciate your support on this."

As time passes, I find I am bringing more energy and creativity to the work I do. My productivity actually increases, and the grumbling from my coworkers gradually subsides. My manager responds well to our conversation, and, in a staff meeting, even talks about how it would be good to see more staff involvement in the community, bringing up my coaching role an example. Soon, I notice more of my coworkers leaving on time so they can participate in volunteer activities at their kids' schools and in their neighborhoods. This brings a tremendous surge of new energy and vitality to the office. My team gets noticed by upper management and wins an award that year for exceeding its goals.

This isn't just a hypothetical. I've seen it happen before, and it can happen in your office. The culture of an entire workplace can change when just one person sets boundaries and holds them firmly.

PART FOUR
Joyful Sharing

THE ISSUE
Gifts are Rarely Free

———————

There was once a monk who kept a book of great value on display in his room. It was written on parchment and bound in gold, and it contained a complete copy of the scriptures—a great rarity in those days. One day, another brother asked if he could borrow the book for a time in order to copy some sections. The first monk picked up the book with a smile and lovingly fingered the engraving on the cover. Then, he told this story:

"When I was a much younger man, this book belonged to a great elder in these parts. I used to see it whenever I went to visit him and ask for his advice. I knew the book was quite valuable, and, to tell you the truth, one day I was overcome by greed. I asked the elder if I could borrow the book in order to study it. Instead, he gave it to me as a gift with this blessing: 'May this book bring you much edification and spiritual growth.'

"The next day, I secretly took the book to a merchant in the nearest town to sell it. The merchant asked if he could keep the book for a day to examine it before agreeing to the price. Knowing that the great elder was very knowledgeable in such matters, he took the book back to its original owner (unbeknownst to him) and said, 'Look, a young man wants to sell me this book. What do you think it is worth?' The elder recognized the book immediately but said nothing. He examined it and said, 'It is worth twice what the seller is asking. Buy it, for it is a good value.'

"The next day, when I went back to see the merchant, he said, 'I took this book to the elder to examine it, and he assured me the price is fair. Here is the money.' Upon hearing this, my heart began to pound, and I started to sweat profusely. My voice shaking, I asked, 'Didn't he say anything else?' The merchant said he did not. I picked up the book with trembling hands and said quietly that I had changed my mind and no longer wished to sell.

"I ran the whole way back to the elder's hut and implored him with tears to take the book back. But he refused. He said, 'I gave the book to you as a free gift with my blessing. Take it, it is yours to do with as you will.' No amount of pleading on my part could convince him to take it back, so I have kept it all these years.

"I must confess to you, in all that time I have never read this book. You see, I never learned how to read. And yet, it has taught me more than I can say."

The monk handed the book to the other brother. "And now, I am giving it to you, freely, and with the same blessing: may it bring you as much edification and spiritual growth as it brought to me."

The Power of Sharing

A gift shared freely, without expectation, has enormous power. It creates a ripple of positive energy in the world—and the effects extend far beyond our limited perception.

The elder in this story offered the book to the brother with the intention that it should be a source of inspiration and spiritual growth. But he did so without tying any expectation to his gift about how that intention would be realized. If the elder had expected the younger monk to grow spiritually by studying the words in the book, he might have gotten upset and taken the book back when he learned the young man was going to sell it for a profit. He might have assumed the gift failed to produce the desired result. I probably would have done just that in his place. I would have felt I was being cheated or made to look foolish.

Very often, we limit the power of our giving by trying to control the outcome. But the elder left his gift free to do its work with quiet confidence that his intention would be realized in due time. He was willing to let the universe surprise him—and it did.

Letting Go of Expectations

I have to be honest: I rarely give anything as freely as this. Instead, I tie expectations to my gifts—little strings that dictate, in my mind, how that gift should be used. For instance, let's say I have a young nephew whose birthday is coming up, and I want to give him an expensive bicycle as a gift. My brother has been out of work for some time, and I know things are tight for his family financially. They can't afford a lot of new things for their children, and I wonder if my nephew Owen feels embarrassed that his clothes and shoes aren't as nice as those of other kids. I think having a really nice bicycle might make him feel less out of place and more at ease with his peers. When I imagine my nephew riding his new bike, I picture the look of pride and joy on his face as he pedals with his friends, his shiny new frame standing out among the group.

In this situation, my intention is that my nephew should feel good about himself and have good relationships with others. My expectation is that riding a fancy bicycle will bring this about. That could happen—but the universe often has other ideas.

When I pull up in the driveway of my brother's house a few weeks later, I am shocked to see Owen riding a bike that is obviously not the one I purchased for him. It is a much simpler and less expensive model, and lacks many of the accessories on the bike I chose. I am full of questions as I get out of the car. Did the bike I purchased get stolen? Did my brother exchange the original bicycle for a cheaper one in order to pay bills? I feel angry and upset, but also sorry for my nephew. I am sure he must be so disappointed to be riding this cheap bicycle instead of the really nice one I bought for him.

When Owen sees me, he immediately rides over to give me a hug. I'm not sure what to say, but my nephew excitedly starts to explain what happened before I can ask. He thanks me for the beautiful bicycle, but admits that he felt a little embarrassed to ride it because it was so much nicer than most of his friends' bikes. He felt especially bad because one of his friends is from a family that can't afford to buy a bicycle for him. So, after talking it over with his parents, he decided to exchange the bicycle I bought for one that cost only half as much and to use the extra money to purchase a bicycle for his friend.

At that moment, my nephew's friend comes riding up on an identical bike. Owen gives me another hug and then rides off with his friend. I can't help but notice the look of incredible pride and joy on his face as I watch him ride.

My intention for my gift was realized, but in a way that was completely contrary to my expectations. My gift unleashed a flow of goodness that went far beyond what I expected, affecting not only Owen, but his friend as well. Who knows how far this current might extend?

THE FIX
Give Your Gift Wings

———————

Joyful Sharing means giving freely of ourselves without becoming entangled in a particular expectation or idea of success. Anytime you want to share something with someone else, whether it is your time, a gift, a special moment, or even just a smile, here are some suggestions for how to share it joyfully:

1. *Create a simple intention* for what you want to share. Your intention could be that you want your gift to be a source of benefit and inspiration to others, or it could be that you want to become a more generous and giving person.

2. *Let go of any expectations* you may have. Resist the inclination to form an image in your mind about what shape success will take. Find joy in the act of sharing itself, not in the outcome.

3. *Release your gift* into the universe, trusting that your intention will be realized, even if you never

know how it happens. Let it go.

4. *Remain open* to a universe of infinite possibilities. Instead of narrowing the field to a limited number of acceptable outcomes, leave room for the surprising and unexpected.

The Two Gates of Joyful Sharing

The First Gate: "No Obligation"

In order for an act of sharing to bring joy into the world, it must meet two tests. I like to picture these tests as gates that each gift must pass through before it is released into the world.

The first gate is called "no obligation." If you or I are giving a gift because we think we have to, it's not really shared freely. Before we give a gift, we must always check ourselves for a sense of obligation, because this can negate the benefit of the gift.

For example, let's say I am a volunteer on a small neighborhood committee in charge of an annual arts and crafts fair at the community center. I know families in the area are excited, and I want the event to live up to their expectations. However, a few committee members keep dropping the ball. I feel obligated to see that everything gets done, so I start taking on more and more of their work until it seems like I'm doing practically everything. I'm miserable, but I don't feel like I have a choice in the matter, and resentment builds against my fellow committee members. Taking on the extra work was ostensibly a gift, but in the long run it did not serve the neighborhood well. I end up ruining my relationships with the other committee members, and decline to participate in any future neighborhood organizing projects, even though I could be a great asset to the community. I acted out of obligation, and my gift turned sour.

When I want to share something of myself with others, the first question I ask is, "Do I feel any sense of obligation about this? Am I doing this grudgingly, because I think I have to?" If the answer is yes, I stop. I have to untie all obligations from my gift before it can pass through the first gate.

For instance, I could have decided to continue my work on the committee but resisted allowing myself to feel responsible for the whole arts fair. My fellow committee members might have stepped up in the absence of my constant over-performance. Even if they didn't, the event likely would have turned out fine—and I would have had the energy to continue serving the neighborhood for years to come.

The Second Gate: "No Expectation"
The second gate through which every act of Joyful Sharing must pass is that of "no expectation." In order to get through this gate, a gift must not be attached to any vision of how it should be used or how the receiver should behave.

Say, for instance, I give a decorative vase to a good friend, just to express how much this person means to me. The next time I go over for a visit, I look all around for the vase, but I don't see it anywhere. Feelings of hurt and resentment arise in me, revealing that I had the expectation that my friend would display the gift as a sign of our friendship. I'm left wondering if our relationship means less to this person than it does to me, and I'm irritated that I spent money and effort on a gift that I think fell flat. Unintentionally, I behave coldly to my friend during our visit, and it's a while before we get together again.

After the gate of "no obligation," I always ask myself, "Do I have a particular expectation about how this will be received? Will I feel angry and resentful if what I give does not achieve a certain outcome?" If the answer to this question is yes, I stop. I have to untie every expectation from my gift before it can pass through the second gate.

If I'd thought about my expectations carefully when I considered buying a vase for my friend, I could have avoided becoming resentful. Perhaps I'd have decided not to give the gift, choosing instead to focus on spending time with this person. Or, maybe I would have been able to let go of my expectations and give freely. Because I didn't do this, my gift damaged our relationship.

When an act of sharing passes through the gates of "no obligation" and "no expectation," it is a free gift, and is ready to be released into the world. A gift like this has tremendous power to bring joy to both the giver and receiver alike.

DEEP DIVE
Like Water from a Well

———————

The universe shares all things freely and unconditionally, without restriction, and all the universe's gifts to us are meant to be shared. As one of the spiritual masters of the Egyptian desert put it, generosity is like a well. When a person does not share, the well slowly silts up from disuse. There is less and less to draw from in the reservoir. Eventually, the aquifer is blocked and the well becomes unusable. We have to draw regularly in order to keep the flow moving. The more we draw, the more productive the well becomes. This may seem paradoxical, but it is quite true. The best reason to give is to keep the current of goodness flowing in our lives by sharing freely what the universe has shared with us.

When I am in touch with this reality, I experience a current of generosity flowing through me that comes from far beyond myself. I know that I am only a channel, and I want to open my heart wide so this stream of goodness can pour into the world.

This is how Joyful Sharing connects us to Purpose. We don't generate the flow. The key is simply not to obstruct it with conditions and expectations. The more restrictions we set on our giving, the more narrow and constricted our lives become, and the less this current is able to move through us.

As we practice Joyful Sharing, it's important to remember that the most powerful gift we have to share is always ourselves—our time, energy, and attention—and not our material possessions. Sharing money and other valuables can be a tangible way of affirming our priorities and cultivating a generous spirit. But it can also be a way of trying to compensate for feelings of guilt when we think we're not sharing enough of ourselves. We see this kind of compensation all the time in families where busy parents buy their children gifts to make up for not spending time with them. But what our children and other loved ones want and need from us more than anything else is our undivided attention and presence. Remember, you are the greatest gift you have to share, and your money and things are a poor stand-in for you.

When we share freely of ourselves in this way, giving and receiving are one and the same. Both are part of the same movement, the same flow. Whatever we give to others—love, kindness, acceptance, understanding—we give to ourselves as well. I have discovered that when I give praise or appreciation to someone else, I have the same warm feeling as if

someone had given it to me. And when I show understanding and acceptance to another person, I feel as
if someone had done the same for me. This means
that whenever I feel unappreciated, misunderstood,
or unloved, the best thing for me to do is to give love,
understanding, and appreciation to someone else,
because we receive whatever we give. In fact, we often
receive even more, because when we allow this kind
of positive energy to flow through us, others are far
more likely to respond in kind.

A Self-Reinforcing Cycle

Giving freely is an inherently joyful act. If we want
more joy in our life, the secret is to give more, with
fewer expectations. We must release our gift into the
world with the sole intention that it should be a source
of positive energy and inspiration, and we must avoid
trying to define what success (or failure) might look
like.

When we want to start practicing Joyful Sharing,
it's helpful to look for very small ways to get started.
The key is to perform little acts of generosity simply
for the joy they bring. When I do this, I find I get so
much joy and happiness in return that I want to do it
again as soon as I can. I start looking for ways to free
up additional resources so that I can give even more
next time.

When we share freely like this, our giving
becomes a self-reinforcing cycle. The more we give,
the more we want to give. Try this for yourself and see

if it isn't true. Do something small to start with. Give five minutes of your undivided attention to a child. Treat a friend for coffee. Give something you don't use to someone who will use it. Opportunities to give will unfailingly show up in your life. Additional time and space will begin to open up, too, and you will have abundant energy and resources to share.

THE MANTRA
I Share What I Have Freely

————————

Learning to give of yourself freely takes time—time, plus one thousand little reminders to let go of the expectations we so naturally attach to our gifts. To help remind myself of my intention to practice Joyful Sharing, I frequently repeat this mantra: *I share what I have freely*. I recommend you try saying this from time to time throughout the day over the next week. Here are some times that I have found this mantra especially useful:

- At the beginning of the workday or any task, as a way of dedicating it to the universe. *I share what I have freely.*

- When I notice I am sharing something grudgingly or reluctantly, out of a sense of obligation. *I share what I have freely.*

- When I catch myself creating expectations or getting stuck in success-or-failure thinking.

I share what I have freely.

- When I feel frustration or resentment because things didn't turn out the way I had planned. *I share what I have freely.*

As you practice Joyful Sharing and use the mantra, you may find your brain resisting the idea of giving without expectation. After all, isn't it okay to have expectations of other people? The answer, of course, is yes. It is perfectly appropriate to have expectations of others, so long as we recognize how these expectations change the nature of our interactions. When we give something with an expectation, we are no longer sharing so much as we are making an exchange. Our giving becomes a transaction, because we are expecting something based on what we give. This is actually more like buying than sharing. We can't experience the joy that comes from generosity and retain control over the outcome at the same time. If I want my giving to be joyful, I have to be willing to surrender my expectations.

The practice of Intentional Welcoming supports and strengthens the practice of Joyful Sharing. After we have been practicing Intentional Welcoming for a while, we have some additional energy and resources at our disposal. We have something worth sharing. Now, by using the mantra for Joyful Sharing, we are making a commitment to share what we have to offer. We can trust the universe is going to present us with new opportunities to do just that. Pay attention so you don't miss these chances.

Intentional Welcoming supports Joyful Sharing in another way as well. If we hold good boundaries and give only when we choose to, this increases our ability to share our gift without any expectation. Freedom begets freedom. If I feel free to give to you when and how I choose, I can more easily allow you the freedom to respond in whatever way you choose. I have noticed that when I'm not holding good boundaries for myself, I am much more likely to tie expectations to what I give. In a twisted way, that strikes me as fair. After all, why should others have the freedom not to live up to my expectations, when I always feel obligated to live up to everybody else's? Only when we hold our limits firmly can we offer our gift freely and without expectation. Then, we are giving because we want to, not because we think we have to.

THE CHALLENGE
Letting Go of Success

———————

"Visualize your success."

We've all heard at least one version of this, likely many.

You might have heard a form of this from a spiritual teacher, someone who believes that mental exercises such as visualizing a desired outcome can engender financial prosperity and other forms of success. Such teachers focus on the power of positive thoughts to get us where we want to go—and of negative thoughts to stop us in our tracks.

Maybe you've heard a variant from a sports coach, a boss, or a mentor. *Imagine yourself hitting the ball. Dress for the job you want. Picture your life in ten years.*

This practice of identifying a vision and focusing on it is deeply ingrained in our success-oriented culture, yet it contains a fatal flaw: our narrow vision of success is probably not the best possible outcome—and will almost always leave us unsatisfied.

We see this all the time. One person might believe marriage is the ultimate goal, the achievement that will bring happiness. Yet, six years into marriage, that person is deeply disappointed. Another person might strive for an executive job with a six-figure salary, only to find the feeling of emptiness cannot be filled with money or prestige.

By carefully crafting visions of success for ourselves, we build a life based on expectations, not intentions. We become governed by a fear of failure, which makes us cautious and timid about how we share our gifts. Instead of giving extravagantly, we hold back, always looking for the sure thing, the guaranteed success. We make safe bets because we don't want to risk wasting our time, energy, and resources. We tackle easy problems instead of hard ones. Fear of failure stifles our willingness to experiment, to try new things if we're not sure they will work. It limits creativity.

As a society, we need people who are willing to take big risks if we want to solve the problems we face today. After all, if we keep doing what we've always done, we'll get the same results we've always had. Bold innovation requires us to let go of self-limiting beliefs about success and failure, to see our experiences as part of a process of learning and growth. In this light, the only real failure is the failure of courage.

If you want to receive, give. If you want to make a difference, give. Don't focus on what you want to get, focus on how you want to share. We've all spent enough years chasing our own vision of success to know it doesn't lead to satisfaction. Instead, we must practice Joyful Sharing. We must focus on our intentions, drawing deeply from the well of generosity, waiting with curiosity to see what the universe has in store.

A Universe of Possibility

Sometimes, we may hold back from giving because we don't believe we have anything worthwhile to share. Maybe your only available time is two hours on Saturday mornings, and you don't think it's enough to make a dent in the cause you care about. Maybe you're a high school dropout, and you're convinced you don't have the smarts or education to offer anything worthwhile. At the core of these kinds of hesitations is a need for our gift to be successful.

You do not have to know the solution to a problem to make a contribution. You do not have to have a PhD to positively influence a child's life. All you have to do is share your gift with the intention that it should be a source of good in the world. When we share freely, the whole universe conspires to support our intention. One act of generosity can unleash a cascade of good effects that were impossible to predict, and it can inspire many others to give in turn, so that the power of our gift is magnified a hundredfold.

So give what you can, even if it seems small. Don't hold back because you think it won't be sufficient to meet the need, and don't be daunted by the fear of failure. Little gifts often turn out to be enough in mysterious and surprising ways. Let it go, and remain open to the infinitely surprising possibilities of the limitless universe.

THE PRACTICE IN PRACTICE
Do With It What You Will

Humor and fun keep a marriage or committed partnership strong and resilient. A couple that can laugh together can weather almost any storm that comes their way. I have noticed that when I am intent on forcing a particular result, I stop having any fun with what I am doing, and all the enjoyment leaches out of the activity. Expectations kill joy, and nowhere is this more true than in committed relationships. Joyful Sharing is about keeping a sense of humor when things don't turn out the way we had expected.

Here's an example of what this might look like. Let's say I have decided to surprise my beloved spouse by making a special dinner. There's no particular occasion, but I haven't been feeling as much closeness as I would like in our marriage, and I want to do something nice for my spouse to help deepen our intimacy. I decide a romantic evening together is just the thing. I get home early so I can cook, set candles on the table, turn down the lights, put on some nice music, and have everything just right for when she arrives.

My spouse gets home tired and a little cranky after a long day at work. Things didn't go so well at the office today, and there's a stressful situation that will have to be dealt with first thing tomorrow morning. The only thing she has in mind for the evening is to get takeout, relax on the couch and watch television, and go to bed early. Seeing candles on the table, my beloved immediately starts feeling on edge. Things only get worse when my spouse realizes what I'm up to. After such a difficult day, my surprise dinner doesn't feel like a loving act—it just feels like one more person expecting her to perform. My beloved gets upset. "How could you do this without telling me?" she asks, irritated. "What did you expect me to say, 'Oh, honey, you shouldn't have'? I can't believe you did this without even asking me!"

My intention was to do something nice for my spouse and foster closeness between us. My expectation was that a romantic dinner would do the trick. But clearly that expectation isn't in line with the reality of her day—regardless of the fact that she's not handling the situation well. I have a choice: I can hold on to the expectation, or I can honor the intention. My natural response is to hold on to the expectation, getting defensive and arguing my spouse should be grateful for what I've done. I could insist we sit down for this nice dinner because I've already gone to so much work. If I respond this way, I will inherently ruin any chance of realizing my intention. We'll probably fight, and both of us will feel resentment toward the other—the exact opposite of my intention.

But that's not my only option. If I honor the intention, all that matters is that my spouse feels loved by me. Instead of getting angry, I turn the music off and put the candles away—without any hint of disappointment or irritation. I declare the dinner I have made "takeout," and together we move it to the coffee table in the living room. I dig out some chopsticks. We eat the meal on the couch, watching my beloved's favorite television show.

My spouse is moved by the fact that I let go of my expectations for the evening and had a sense of humor about things. We talk about what happened that day and the situation that has to be dealt with at the office the next morning. We end up having a really nice evening together, and the experience brings us closer. We laugh about this story for years afterward. My expectation for the evening did not turn out as I had planned, but my intention of strengthening our relationship was accomplished in a lovelier way than I could have foreseen.

Beyond Success and Failure

Joyful Sharing is the key to creativity and innovation. By shaping life around our intentions instead of expectations, we leave room for experimentation and surprise twists. We have no reason to fear failure, because we have no set vision of success. In fact, sometimes it's hard to tell the difference.

Say a friend of mine and I have an idea to start a company together in a field we're both passionate about. We identify some "angel" investors who provide startup capital, then hire a small staff and start product development. We spend the next several years working long hours, but it appears to be worth it: we've got a superb internal culture with a great team dynamic.

Despite delivering a good product on schedule, however, our company struggles to gain market share and get to scale. Unexpected shifts in market conditions diminish demand for our product, and some new entrants provide stronger-than-expected competition. We give it our all, but, after a few years, my co-founder and I decide to call it quits. The company fails. It's a difficult and emotional time. Our investors end up losing some of their money, which leads to some very tense and difficult negotiations toward the end. We have to lay off the entire staff, and tears are shed when my business partner and I turn off the lights for the last time and lock the doors for good.

By our culture's standards, this is a story about failure. But is it, really? Despite going through some very difficult times, my co-founder and I remain good friends. In fact, we grow even closer through the process. My partner goes on to start a highly profitable venture with another collaborator, and he credits his success to the lessons learned from our experience. I stay in touch with many of my former employees, several of whom have gone on to important leadership roles in other companies. Some of them call me when confronted with big decisions, and I end up becoming something of an informal mentor to several of them. I enjoy this role so much that, eventually, I establish my own successful career coaching business. Although the original company did not last, it enabled me to discover my passion for helping people develop themselves and realize their full potential.

In this story, where does failure end and success begin? If my business partner and I orient our lives around expectations, then closing our company would have been an undeniable failure. We might even have come to resent one another or our employees, feeling that we gave of ourselves without proper reward. But if we orient ourselves around our intentions, we can't help but see the whole story as a winding path to surprising fulfillment. We each intended to become financially secure through a job we enjoyed, to connect to Purpose through our work.

In the long run, our dreams came true.

PART FIVE
Grateful Receiving

THE ISSUE
Gray-Tinted Glasses

———————

Once there was a spiritual community of brothers who lived together in the desert and shared a common life. They all ate the same food, wore the same robes, and slept on the same kind of straw mattress.

Among these brothers, there was one who was always complaining. He complained about the food, about the clothing, about the living quarters. Nothing was good enough for him. The rest of the monks didn't like to be around him, so he ate all of his meals alone. One night, as the community gathered for dinner, someone he didn't know sat down next to him. Immediately, the complaining brother started prattling about the lousy food. His companion listened for a while, then said, "Tell me friend, what did you do before you joined this community?"

"I was a shepherd," the unhappy monk said, "and I had a very difficult life. I used to sleep outside on the ground, with no roof over my head. When it was very cold, I would lie shivering under my thin blanket. I desperately wanted to shear a couple of sheep to make myself a good woolen blanket, but I knew the owner of the sheep would beat me if any of his wool went missing. Often, there wasn't enough food, and I would go hungry for days at a time. I was so tempted to slaughter one of the sheep, but again, I knew the owner would beat me."

"So your life here is much better than it was before, is it not?" the second brother asked. "You have a roof over your head, a warm bed, and meals every day."

"Well, yes," the dour monk admitted grudgingly. "That's true. But things could be much better than they are now. The cooks are always ruining the food, the beds are uncomfortable, and the clothes don't ever seem to fit right. If I were running this place, things would be different."

They ate in silence for a while, and the complaining brother started to wonder about his companion. Finally, he asked, "What about you? What was your life like before you came to this place?"

The second brother put down his fork and looked at the first with a smile. "I was a high-ranking official in the imperial palace. There, I had servants who attended to my every need. I ate the finest delicacies every day, dressed in tailored clothing and slept in a soft bed with silk sheets." The complaining brother was speechless. Finally, he blurted, "What on earth brought you here? What would make you leave all that for this?"

"Ah," replied the second, "I came here to find the secret of happiness. You see, I was never satisfied with what I had when I lived in the palace. I found fault with everything, and I always wanted more. But since I came here and learned the secret, food has never tasted so good. I sleep like a baby at night, and my clothing is perfectly satisfactory, even if it's a little ill-fitting."

No one had mentioned the secret of happiness to the unappreciative brother before. He looked around to make sure no one else was listening, lowered his voice, and asked, "Can you tell me the secret?"

"It's easier if I show you." The second brother got up from the table and walked over to the cook, who looked harried and exhausted after preparing dinner for so many. He clasped the cook by the hand, looked him in the eye, and said, "Thank you for the wonderful supper. It was delicious. I enjoyed it very much." Immediately, the cook lit up. His face brightened, his slumped shoulders straightened, and he beamed at the brother, who smiled back at him warmly.

Then he looked over at the complaining monk and winked.

The Secret of Happiness

Gratitude is the secret of happiness.

The second monk knew it. He'd left behind immense material wealth and power, yet he found happiness in uninspired cuisine and a straw mattress.

Maybe you know it—but only at a theoretical level. You tell your children or your friends to be grateful, but, internally, your mind keeps an ongoing tally of things that aren't the way you'd like. Perhaps, in conversation, you default to talking about the ways relationships or situations aren't ideal. Maybe you do this artfully, so it doesn't sound like complaining, framing your qualms as personal challenges or concern for others. This is certainly true of me. I find fault with what I have, and I want what I don't have. I complain about my situation to myself, to other people, maybe even to God or the universe.

Complaining never helps. It only reaffirms my negative mindset and makes me feel worse about my situation. Even when I do get what I want, I usually don't feel any better. The truth is, we are poor predictors of our own happiness, and the things we think will make us happy often don't. Like the complaining brother, I soon find a new reason to be dissatisfied. After all, when you go through life wearing gray-tinted glasses, everything looks dreary.

But, as the grateful brother discovered, the secret to happiness works in any situation, whether we have a lot or just a little. No matter our circumstances, there is always something to be grateful for. Sometimes a loss or setback can actually help us better appreciate what we do have: family, friends, community, relationships. In times like these, we can learn to value what matters most, and find joy in simple pleasures like the grateful brother did. In fact, sometimes not getting what we want turns out to be the greatest gift of all.

For instance, let's say I was just passed over for a promotion at work that I thought I truly deserved. A friend of mine, a colleague who is my junior by a couple of years, was moved into the position instead. I'm upset with my boss for not noticing the extra work I've been putting in lately. I'm pretty angry with my colleague as well; I feel somehow betrayed that a friend would take a position that I had so clearly earned. I don't think my colleague is as qualified as I am, and I can't help but wonder if something happened behind my back.

In a situation like this, it would be easy for me to become bitter and start complaining, thinking that I was deprived of something that was rightfully mine—a downward spiral that leads nowhere good.

Instead, I decide to intentionally reassess the situation, looking for the gift it contains. I request a meeting with my boss and respectfully explain that I was disappointed not to get the promotion. I ask for feedback about how to improve my performance in the future so I'll have a better shot at getting promoted next time. In the process, I learn some surprising things about myself.

My boss explains that while my performance is completely satisfactory, over the past year I seem to have lost passion for the work. Some of my coworkers have remarked that I seem apathetic and disinterested. My boss assumed I was looking to move on, and was surprised I applied for an internal promotion.

If I can take this feedback well, it's incredibly useful information. I clearly need to reflect on my attitude. Maybe I become a much more valuable asset to the company and advance rapidly thanks to this experience. Maybe I decide it's time for a bigger challenge and leap to a new career that excites me.

In the end, getting passed over for the promotion was a huge disappointment—and a powerful turning point in my career. It's all in how I choose to receive it.

THE FIX
Changing Our Lenses

—————

Finding the gems hidden in difficult experiences is the heart of Grateful Receiving. This spiritual practice invites us to creatively reappraise our current situation in order to discover the gift it contains. Here are some simple suggestions for making Grateful Receiving a part of your life today:

1. *Pause for a moment* to consider what you have to be thankful for. Take a gratitude break.

2. *Take inventory* of what you appreciate about your life right now. What are the unacknowledged favors or "gifts in disguise" that you may not have recognized? Come up with two or three things. You may want to write them down.

3. *Focus your attention* on these bright spots. Instead of concentrating on problems, focus on what's going right.

4. *Express gratitude.* Remember to say "thank you"

to other people and/or the universe for what you have received. When you do this, you will feel happier. Try it and see if it isn't true.

Gratitude Jump Start: A Two-Part Exercise

Part One: The Gratitude Short List

If you want to infuse your daily life with a renewed sense of appreciation, you need a "gratitude jump start." This is an exercise I use personally, and it has a dramatic effect on my happiness.

The first part of the exercise is to write down one to three key bright spots in your life. Think of this as a "gratitude short list." What is going right? Who hasn't let you down lately? Here are some things I came up with when I did this exercise:

- I am grateful for my health.

- I am grateful for the support of my spouse.

- I am grateful for the chance to see an old friend recently.

Don't fret about only writing down the three things for which you are most thankful. The point is simply to have a short list of things you appreciate. I prefer short lists to long ones because they allow for more focus and clarity.

Part Two: Expressing Appreciation

Once you've come up with your gratitude short list, it's time to express appreciation.

I know. This is uncomfortable for some of you.

Really uncomfortable. But it's not enough to simply identify what we are grateful for—we have to actually say "thank you" in order for the process to really take. The act of showing appreciation increases the flow of gratitude in our lives and can produce a flood of new reasons to be grateful.

If you can, it's always best to do this in person. If that's not an option, you can also make a call or send a text, an email, or a letter. Don't make this too complicated; keep your expressions of gratitude short and focused. At some point in your conversation with this person, use a few words to convey your appreciation for their contribution in your life. This could be as simple as saying, "You have always been there for me when I needed you. Thank you."

If you want to express gratitude to someone who has passed away or is otherwise no longer in your life, consider writing a short note of thanks and then "sending" it in some creative way, such as burning or burying it. If you're showing appreciation to the universe, just call to mind what you are grateful for, and then whisper "thank you" out loud. The universe will know what you mean.

This practice may seem awkward and insincere to you at first. You may not feel particularly grateful when you say the words. You might even feel grouchy about doing it. That's okay. The key is to keep practicing every day. Smile, even if you have to force it a little. Remember that gratitude and appreciation are not feelings at all—they are intentional practices. Like compassion, gratitude is a habit and a skill that we learn by repetition.

I promise, if you practice gratitude regularly in this way, feelings of happiness, contentment, and satisfaction will soon follow.

DEEP DIVE
No One is Self-Made

_____

Life is a precious gift that no one does anything to deserve. Nobody earns the right to be born. We all come into the world empty-handed.

Grateful Receiving connects us to Purpose through awareness that everything we have is a gift from the universe. There are no truly "self-made" people. We are who we are because of caregivers, teachers, mentors, and countless others along the way who supported and believed in us. We stand on the shoulders of the generations before us, who gave us our language, culture, technology, and so much more.

Gratitude situates us in a universe of connections. Ingratitude, on the other hand, is profoundly isolating. When we are ungrateful, we cut ourselves off from everyone and everything, imagining that we acquired what we have solely on the basis of our own merits. We act as if we had it coming to us, as if life owed us something. Ingratitude is a lonely way to live.

It separates us from other people, and it disconnects us from Purpose as well.

The Power of Forgiveness

When I don't get what I want or what I think I deserve, bitterness often seeps in. It's a sour taste in my mouth, a scowl on my face, resentment in my gut.

One of the spiritual masters of the Egyptian desert said bitterness is like a mouthful of blood: better to spit it out than to swallow it. When people don't live up to our expectations or life doesn't turn out the way we planned, it's natural to feel angry and disappointed. But if we hold on to these feelings by telling ourselves the same story over and over—*I was wronged, I was cheated, I was taken advantage of*—they eventually sour into bitterness.

Bitterness is like acid. It dissolves everything it touches. It eats away at happiness, contentment, affection, well-being. It destroys marriages, ruins friendships, turns members of the same family against each other. Bitterness consumes gratitude. It makes us caustic to everyone around us.

When I notice bitterness seeping into my life, I know to use an antidote—and fast. The treatment is simple, but highly effective. I call to mind a short maxim: "Life owes me nothing." I remember that life itself is an undeserved gift from the universe. Meditating on this truth neutralizes corrosive bitterness.

Another word for this act of letting go is

forgiveness. When we realize that life owes us nothing, we can forgive other people and the universe for not providing everything we want. We don't do this for the sake of the person who has angered us, but for our own sake, because we know bitterness will destroy everything good and beautiful and joyous in our life.

Forgiveness means choosing gratitude.

THE MANTRA
I Receive the Gift That Is Offered

———————

Practicing Grateful Receiving on a daily basis requires returning, again and again, to the reality that life owes us nothing. That gratitude is a practice, not a feeling. That anything can be a gift if we choose to see it that way. To help me remember these things, I repeat the following mantra: *I receive the gift that is offered*. I recommend saying it from time to time throughout the day for the next week. Here are some times I have found this mantra particularly helpful:

- When I want to express appreciation for something wonderful, like the smile on my child's face. *I receive the gift that is offered.*

- When something comes into my life that doesn't feel like a gift, such as a difficult person or a painful experience. *I receive the gift that is offered.*

- When I notice I'm taking things for granted, or

when I can't think of anything for which I am grateful. *I receive the gift that is offered.*

- When I recognize that bitterness is seeping into my life because I missed out on something I thought I deserved. *I receive the gift that is offered.*

By now, you know what a mantra is: a bargain with the universe. So when you use this mantra, you are committing to receive whatever gifts the universe offers, and you should be prepared for some surprises. Pay attention so you don't miss any gifts in disguise. I have found that if I refuse to accept a gift when it is offered the first time, it often shows up again and again in different forms. A gift like this might present itself more and more insistently until I finally recognize and receive it for what it is.

As you practice Grateful Receiving and use the mantra, you might hear a voice in your head objecting: "Am I really supposed to feel grateful for *everything*?" I have certainly asked myself this question. After all, many situations are hard to feel thankful for. Some are so painful and distressing that it's difficult to imagine any upside. Take heart. Not every experience is recognizable as a gift, at least not right away. Some take years. Some may take a lifetime. Some more than that. We may never be able to understand why certain things happen to us or people we care about. You don't have to be thankful for something that doesn't seem like a gift. Just keep looking for little things that you do feel grateful for right now.

I have found that if I focus on small acts of gratitude, larger questions often seem to take care of themselves. The practice of Grateful Receiving isn't about suddenly and magically feeling grateful for everything all at once. It's about slowly growing in gratitude, finding a bit more to appreciate every day.

THE CHALLENGE
The Gift of Difficult People

———

There is an old story from the Egyptian desert about a female hermit, known as an anchoress, who was walking down a dirt road on her way to a nearby town to sell ropes and baskets. Along the way, she met a woman sitting by the side of the road who complained that she had been abandoned by her traveling companions while she slept. She asked the anchoress where she was going, and, when the anchoress told her which town, she asked if she could come along. The anchoress agreed, and they walked together.

The anchoress soon realized why the woman's companions had snuck away in the middle of the night. She was incredibly disagreeable and argumentative. No matter what the anchoress said, her new companion found a reason to contradict it. Things only got worse when they got to the town. The woman sat down next to the anchoress in the market and argued with people who came by, chasing away customer after customer. When the anchoress finally sold a few items, the woman demanded they split the proceeds, claiming that people had only bought the goods because of her expert salesmanship.

At the end of the day, the anchoress had little to show for her efforts. As she gathered up her unsold wares, the woman got up to follow, saying she needed to retrieve the rest of her belongings from camp. They walked together in the direction from which they had come, the woman still waving her arms and carrying on one-sided arguments with people they had left behind in the marketplace hours before. The light was dim by the time they arrived at the spot where they had first met. The anchoress said goodbye to the woman, but, as she began to walk away, she heard a voice behind her saying, "You are blessed. You are blessed. You are blessed." She turned around, but no one was there. The woman had disappeared.

The anchoress decided it must have been an angel from heaven sent to teach her patience.

Difficult people can be our greatest teachers in the spiritual life. Each day, I try to think of every person who comes into my life as a gift. I do my best to act as if it were true, regardless of whether the person feels like a gift. Sometimes, the gift the other person offers is the opportunity to become more patient and understanding. Sometimes, it's the chance to learn how to say no and mean it, to become stronger in the face of criticism, or to stand up for myself and hold my ground. Without difficult or demanding people, we might never learn these important skills. We might not discover our own inner strength, fierceness, and resolve.

For instance, let's say I'm on a committee to plan an event for my child's school. One of the other members, Jan, has a very forceful personality. Jan wants to charge admission to help pay for some needed classroom upgrades. I think the event should remain free so everyone can come. Every time I try to share my point of view, however, I get steamrolled.

Instead of getting angry and resentful, I could reappraise the situation and try to see Jan as a gift. This is an opportunity for me to learn how to speak up for myself and not be so easily intimidated or shut down. In the process of learning to speak louder and stand my ground, I might even start to feel some admiration for Jan's strength of personality.

In the end, we keep admission free but sell raffle tickets to raise money. The event goes beautifully, and even better, Jan and I become friends. As time goes on, I find that I am more and more thankful for the gift she is to me: someone who challenges me to grow stronger and isn't afraid to tell me when I might be making a mistake.

Spinning Straw into Gold

Many cultures have fables about spinning straw into gold or weaving cotton into silk—taking what is apparently of little worth and turning it into something extraordinarily valuable.

When we practice Grateful Receiving, this is exactly what we are doing. Gratitude transforms everything. Difficult experiences that once seemed like hardships we now recognize as opportunities. People we might previously have regarded as annoyances or irritants we now see as teachers, even angels. Even our darkest and most painful moments can turn into valuable gifts of wisdom and insight that we can share with others. Where someone else might see only a pile of worthless straw, we can point to it and say, "Look at all this gold in the making!" That's the power of gratitude.

THE PRACTICE IN PRACTICE
Gratitude Connects Us

————

The universe does not give us anything so we can keep it for ourselves. Whatever the universe offers is given for one reason only: to be shared with others. In no case is this more true than the gift of painful experiences. As strange as it may sound, these experiences frequently contain hidden gifts that we can share with other people. I have often found that until I've had a certain experience, I am prone to think, "That could never happen to me." I consider myself too smart, too talented, too healthy, too organized—you name it. In other words, I think I'm pretty special.

The gift of painful experiences is *ordinariness*—the realization that we are not so different from other people after all. And this is a profoundly good thing. We can relate to others in ways we could never have imagined before we had the experience. We can ask for and receive help from other people. And after coming through the experience, we have something valuable to share: wisdom. We can help people who are in similar situations by offering our own experience and insight, and we can give them hope that they will not always be stuck where they are now.

Say I am going through a series of painful circumstances, such as a divorce and subsequent separation from my children, and I sink into a serious depression. I feel tired all the time, and things that used to give me pleasure just don't excite me anymore. I find it hard to get out of bed in the morning because I feel like I don't have anything to wake up for. Sometimes, I start to wonder if life is even worth living. I've always thought of people who committed suicide as weak, and up to now I considered myself strong and self-sufficient, so I have a hard time asking for help. I never thought something like this would happen to me.

Fortunately, I have a strong support network—friends and family members who rally around me during this difficult time. It's humbling to admit that I can't do this on my own, that I need help. But this admission brings with it a flood of support and positive energy. With the encouragement of family and friends, I go to see my doctor, find a therapist, and start taking medication. I begin to understand my own thinking better, and my therapist helps me identify self-defeating thought patterns that lead to feelings of worthlessness and shame. Slowly, I start feeling better, though it takes longer than I expected. I begin to notice there are things in my life I am looking forward to, opportunities I want to live for.

An experience like this can be a hard pill to swallow, and some may fall into addictions or other self-destructive behaviors as they seek relief from the pain.

Yet just imagine the beauty that could come from my circumstances. My relationships can strengthen. I can absorb lessons about marriage that lead to a happy and secure second partnership. I can grow those first rays of excitement into lifelong passions.

Most of all, I can learn to embrace the gift of an ordinary life. If I remain open, I'll see that I'm not so different from anyone else—that I'm not strong while they are weak. After this experience, I can relate to people who are struggling, and share deeply personal stories that might be an encouragement to them.

It just might turn out to be the worst and best thing that ever happened to me.

Using Our Imagination

When I just can't seem to find anything to feel thankful for, I have discovered some imaginative techniques that are incredibly helpful in rekindling gratitude. For instance, I might close my eyes and imagine that I am on a spaceship orbiting the planet. There has been a terrible accident—the spaceship has veered off course, and I have just learned that there is no way to turn it around. There is enough food, water, and oxygen on board to sustain me, but I will not be returning to Earth. I watch through a window in the spacecraft as our lovely blue planet gets smaller and smaller. In that moment, I would give anything just to breathe fresh air again, feel the breeze on my face, and walk in the cool grass with my bare feet. If I could do this even one more time, I would think I was in paradise.

Then, I open my eyes and discover that all these gifts are miraculously available to me right now. I am in paradise.

Our problem is that we don't usually recognize these gifts for what they really are. We take them for granted. Using a mental exercise like this can help us enjoy and appreciate the miracles that are all around us.

The enemy of gratitude is over-familiarity. Often, the greatest gifts in our lives are the things we take most for granted. They are like wallpaper—we see them so often we have stopped noticing them. The support of a committed partner or spouse, the simple joy of playing with a child, the flavor of food, the relief of cool water—use your imagination to redis-cover miracles like these. What would happen if you lost your sense of taste? Instead of looking forward to meals, eating would become a chore, something you had to do to stay alive. If you could taste your food again after such an experience, how differently would you eat your meals? I know I would chew much more slowly, savoring every mouthful.

If we take this exercise a step further and imag-ine where we would be if we lost someone important to us, we might even trigger some real feelings of grief. Heartfelt Listening helps us remember why those feelings are there in the first place: to remind us of what is most precious in life before it's too late. Whenever I consider such a loss, I immediately want to go and tell the people I love just how much they mean to me and show how much I appreciate them. We have the chance to do this every day for those closest to us, but often we don't take advantage of the opportunity. That's what makes these imaginative techniques so powerful: they refresh our perspective, helping us to stop taking the people we care about for granted and start expressing our appreciation to them right now, while we still have time.

THE ISSUE
Defaulting to Iron

———————

There once was a young hunter who left his life of independence to join a spiritual community. This man had a very difficult time adjusting to community life. As a hunter, he had lived a solitary existence, often spending days at a time alone in the wilderness. He had made his own choices. But in the community he was constantly around other people, and there was often tension between various personalities. This was especially true when decisions had to be made that affected all the brothers. Inevitably, someone did not get their way, and the new brother felt frustrated when that someone turned out to be him.

After some time, the abbot of the community took the new brother aside for a walk and asked him about his former life. "Tell me," said the abbot, "when you were a hunter, how did you choose the material to make your bow?" The brother, who had been quite sullen and morose up to this point, cheered up immediately and began to explain the qualities of different kinds of wood: "I always used yew for my bows, because it's the strongest and most resilient of the woods, much better than larch or cedar. A yew bow is incredibly powerful. With it, my arrows would fly far and still land true."

The abbot nodded, and then asked, "If you were aiming for power, why not make your bow out of iron? Surely iron is stronger than yew?"

"Iron is strong, that's true," said the new brother, furrowing his brow, "but it lacks resilience. You can't bend an iron bow. It doesn't have the flexibility you need, so you can't get the proper tension out of it. It's just too rigid. You wouldn't be able to draw such a bow, and even if you could, it would probably just snap in two."

"I see," said the abbot. Then he looked the new brother square in the eye and said, "Son, like your bow, all the power in human relationships lies in the tension between two points. Places like this community are full of tension, but they are full of great power as well. No one wants to bend or give up their own way; that's just human nature. But I have learned that when I yield, that's when I am really strong. Where the tension is the greatest, that's where the arrow flies the farthest."

The Power of Yielding

With this simple image, the wise abbot was able to capture one of the most important lessons about human relationships, and to do so in a language the new brother could easily understand. Like a bow when it is bent, we generate power when we yield. When we give a little in our relationships, when we are willing to compromise and open to the influence of others, we create a dynamic and fruitful tension.

This lesson may seem simple, but it is extremely difficult to live by. I hate it when I don't get my way. Like the new brother, I want things how I want them and get upset when my wishes are thwarted. When I insist on having my own way, everything becomes a contest of wills: I win if I get what I want, I lose if I don't. This kind of mental rigidity, however, doesn't get me very far. I get stuck in recurring patterns of behavior, thinking the same old thoughts and doing the same old things. Inflexibility produces no power.

Yet inflexibility is often perceived as strength. We know this is true on a national scale. In politics, "compromise" has become a bad word, and disagreeing factions are digging their heels into the ground. If we're honest, this is true in our personal life as well. We're slow to concede a point to our partner or spouse in a disagreement, and we're more interested in converting a colleague to our idea than crafting a compromise.

For example, let's say my partner and I are having frequent disagreements about how to manage our money. My partner is very careful about spending. She keeps a record of all purchases, reconciles them at the end of each month, and then compares them to our budget to be sure our spending stays within limits. I, on the other hand, am much more relaxed when it comes to money and finances. I like buying gifts for other people and splurging on special occasions. I have a tendency to lose track of my spending, and sometimes I overspend on our budget. I often don't save receipts from purchases, and I don't like taking the time every month to reconcile the accounts.

Money is a source of continuous friction between us. When we go on vacation, my partner worries about money, while I just want to relax and have a good time. My partner gets really upset when we overspend our budget or can't account for certain expenditures. I get tense and defensive whenever the subject comes up. I argue that there are much more important concerns in the world than being a few dollars over on our grocery budget. I say money doesn't matter all that much anyway, and hint that if my partner was more spiritually-minded like I am, we wouldn't be having this argument all the time.

The tension between me and my partner on this subject is extremely difficult for many couples to resolve. But what if the point isn't to resolve the tension at all, but rather to draw on it as a source of energy for generating personal growth?

If I can lower my defenses a little bit, it will be plain to me that I have room to grow in the area of money management. I want things my way, and I'm resistant to my spouse's efforts to rein in my spending. Worse, I'm cloaking this in spiritual language in an attempt to make myself look superior.

But secretly, I may actually appreciate my partner's efforts to keep our spending in line. I admire my partner's discipline when it comes to finances, and am grateful that I never have to worry that there might not be enough money in the account for all our bills, which used to happen to me sometimes before we got together.

If I can let my guard down a little, my partner may also be willing to admit that there are some positive aspects to how I approach money. We might even agree that there are worse things in the world than going a few dollars over budget on our groceries.

If both sides feel safe in the conversation, we can each confess that there are things we admire and appreciate about the other's way of thinking about money—and out of that could come powerful personal growth and a more united approach to spending. But in order for this to happen, we have to stop fighting to get our own way.

THE FIX
Respecting Tension

Drawing on the tension in our relationships as a source of energy for transformation is the basis of Cooperative Building, the last and highest of the Six Spiritual Practices. Cooperative Building means gracefully partnering with others to construct a new way of living together. These are the basic steps:

1. *Observe the tension* that builds whenever someone proposes an idea that is different from your own. You might notice your muscles tensing, your body stiffening, your chest tightening, or your jaw clenching. Don't resist or try to change anything at first, just recognize the tension for what it is: energy manifesting in your body.

2. *Lower your defenses.* Instead of becoming oppositional or fighting what the other person is proposing, make a conscious effort to relax into the tension and let down your guard. You can

reestablish a sense of safety by reminding yourself that the other person is a partner and collaborator, not an enemy.

3. *Engage a playful mindset.* Playfulness is just another word for flexibility, a supple quality of the mind that converts tension into energy for change. Without making any commitments, try the other person's ideas on for size—"just for fun," so to speak. Give yourself permission to play with an approach that is different from your own.

4. *Focus on the process* rather than the product or outcome. Gently set aside any rigid ideas you may have about how things should turn out; you can always go back to them later. Instead, redirect your attention to the cooperative endeavor, anticipating that something new and unexpected is about to emerge.

The Two Aspects of Cooperative Building

Cooperative Building can reshape our notions about what it means to help other people. Frequently, what we think of as "helping" others involves a power imbalance, as if help is something the strong do for the weak or the well-off do for the needy. This kind of approach is inherently disempowering for those being helped. Real power lies not in the helper or the helped, but in the space between—in the very act of coming together. When we engage in processes that are truly cooperative instead of one-sided, we are helping each other develop to our full human potential.

The First Aspect: Receiving Help Gracefully

The practice of Cooperative Building has two aspects, which are like the sides of a coin: they are the same reality viewed from two different angles. You can't have one without the other. The first aspect of Cooperative Building is *receiving help gracefully*. We must ask for help and be willing to accept it. This involves letting go of the idea that I can do everything myself. So long as I am determined to have things my own way, I won't be willing to let other people in or consider their approaches. I'll stay stuck in my own way of doing things.

When we request assistance from others, we are making ourselves vulnerable, which can feel quite scary. But asking for help is actually a form of power. After all, clinging to our own way of doing things at all costs, even when it's not working for us, is the very definition of weakness. Strength, on the other hand, is inviting others to help us improve on our ideas. Things may not turn out exactly how we had originally planned, but something even better may emerge through the process.

This kind of vulnerability requires courage. We are taking a risk by admitting that we need support, that we can't do everything on our own. Think back for a moment to the tension between me and my partner over our spending habits. What would happen if I asked my partner to help me become a better money manager? I would have to be willing to expose my limitations and affirm her strengths. But in the process, I would become stronger and more complete as a human being.

When I notice that I am resistant to taking these kinds of risks, sometimes it helps to gently ask myself, "What's the worst that could happen? How bad could it be to get some fresh ideas and a different perspective?" I remind myself that I can always go back to doing things my own way if I don't like what other people have to offer. This is the kind of playful mindset that generates power for change.

The Second Aspect: Offering Help Respectfully

The second aspect of Cooperative Building is *offering help respectfully*. This means providing assistance to others in such a way that we do not impose our own will on them or take away their freedom and initiative.

I have often noticed that in situations where I think someone needs my help, I have a tendency to play the hero. I want to jump in and save the day. Instead of working cooperatively with the other person, I immediately start trying to do everything for them. What I am really doing is building myself up at the expense of the one I am supposedly attempting to help. As a result, that person may feel incompetent or inadequate, and become more and more dependent on my assistance.

The most effective kind of help we can ever offer someone else is to let them shine, to reflect back to them just how capable and talented we think they really are. We can do this by affirming their gifts and helping them maximize their strengths. Most importantly, we have to support their ability to come to their own conclusions and make their own choices, even when we disagree with them.

Helping others is a powerful act, but not if we use it as a way to exercise power over them. If we do this, they are likely to resist, and a power struggle will ensue between us. Oftentimes, I feel absolutely certain that other people's lives would be much better if I could just run them for a little while. When I see others making choices I strongly disagree with, there is an immediate temptation to want to "grab the wheel." Under the guise of offering "help," I end up vying for control of the outcome with the other person.

Whenever I notice that I am starting to get into a power struggle with someone else, I take that as a signal that I need to step back and start practicing Cooperative Building. I make a conscious effort to relax into the tension and focus on the collaborative process instead of fixating on the product. I remember that as I am helping others, they are also helping me. Together, we are unfolding toward our life's true Purpose.

DEEP DIVE
The New Human Community

As we practice Cooperative Building, we realize that nothing depends entirely on our own efforts. All creation is *co-creation*. This teaches us to value the contributions of other people, even if they seem at first to be in opposition to our own ideas. When we are willing to be flexible and work with others in our decision-making process, something magical happens. There is a hidden genius that is released from the tension in our relationships, like a genie from a bottle. The ancients had a word for this kind of magic: they called it *synergism*. This term refers to the power that is generated when two different elements combine to create an effect that is greater than either would have had separately.

Synergism is a form of alchemy, and nowhere is its potency more evident than in the alchemy of human relationships. So long as we cling to our own ideas simply because they are ours, nothing happens; our efforts remain static and inert. But when we are willing to give up on having things our way and instead come together with others in a spirit of cooperation, a creative force is unleashed. A powerful dynamism takes over whenever we combine our efforts and ideas with those of other people.

The deeper we go in this practice, the more we discover that we are cooperating not only with other people, but with the universe as well. Little by little, the universe is orchestrating the emergence of a new kind of human community, a more collaborative way of living together. To the extent that we stay pliant in our thinking and open to others' input, we participate in this universal movement toward a more cooperative future.

Cooperative Building is the capstone of the Six Practices. It builds on all the other Practices, especially Joyful Sharing and Grateful Receiving. In the new way of living together we are seeking to co-construct, everyone will have a contribution to make, and each person's contribution will be uniquely valued. Likewise, everyone will have something to receive from others, something to appreciate and feel grateful for. In this way, the distinction between "helpers" and "helped," between designated givers and receivers, will gradually diminish and disappear. Instead of the strong helping the weak or the well-off helping the needy, we will all be helping each other flourish. This process will encompass everyone—not just the people who look, think, act, or talk like us.

This new human community will harness and benefit from the fully realized potential of every individual. All the resources we need will be at our disposal. In our current situation, so much of our potential is being drained away by poverty, addiction, violence, lack of opportunity, and hopelessness. These unfortunate realities stunt our growth and degrade our capability as a human community. We need every person operating at their full capacity to confront the great challenges that face humanity: eradicating disease, ending poverty, decoding the mysteries of the brain and the human genome, exploring and inhabiting the cosmos.

Creating this new community is the great human task, the highest expression of Purpose.

THE MANTRA

I Co-Create a New Reality

———————

The mantra for Cooperative Building invites us to draw upon the synergism in our relationships. It's a phrase that, for me, helps release the dynamism in tension and generate power for personal and community transformation. The sixth mantra goes like this: *I co-create a new reality.* I invite you to try saying this mantra several times a day over the next week. You can use the mantra anytime, but here are some situations where I find this mantra particularly helpful:

- When I am engaged in a cooperative process with someone else and I notice that synergism is starting to flow. *I co-create a new reality.*

- When I am feeling resistance to asking for help or fear of making myself vulnerable. *I co-create a new reality.*

- When I am feeling the urge to "grab the wheel" from someone else and make their decisions for them. *I co-create a new reality.*

- Anytime I am starting to get locked in a power struggle with another person. *I co-create a new reality.*

When we use this mantra, we are signaling our readiness to partner with the universe in constructing a new kind of community, but we shouldn't expect that we will suddenly start getting along with everyone. If anything, you may notice that the tension in your relationships actually increases. This isn't a sign that something is wrong. Remember what the wise abbot said: tension is just energy for transformation. The universe is taking you up on your offer.

As you practice using this final mantra, you may notice some skepticism arising. All this talk about a "new reality" might start to sound a little far-fetched. I have to confess that I have felt this way at times. There have been situations where I have tried to practice Cooperative Building and attempted to use the mantra, and afterwards it seemed like nothing happened. I didn't feel any synergism, and things appeared to go on exactly the way they did before. Then a voice in my head tells me, "Don't kid yourself. It's a dog-eat-dog world out there. Nothing new ever really happens." A voice like this is a kind of self-fulfilling prophecy; if we believe it, then it will surely come true.

When I hear this voice, I don't try to argue with it. I simply name it for what it is: fear of disappointment. I am afraid of being let down, and I'm trying to protect myself from pain. Then, I gently remind myself to have a little patience. After all, the emergence of something new is often invisible in the early stages. It may seem as if nothing is happening, but the deeper truth may be that something is growing. Every time we engage in cooperative efforts instead of competing for raw dominance, we are taking one small step toward the creation of a new kind of human community. This process doesn't happen all at once. It unfolds slowly, almost imperceptibly, like a seed germinating in darkness beneath the surface of the soil.

The next thing I do when I notice skepticism arising is to engage hope. It's important to understand what this word actually means. People sometimes use it to express a preference for something they feel powerless to attain, as in, "I hope things get better for you someday," or "I hope it doesn't rain tomorrow." But this is not really what hope is about. Hope is not a feeble wish that things should change, it is a catalyst that creates the very conditions in which change is possible. Far from starry-eyed optimism, hope is a fierce and ardent resolve with the power to transform any situation. Hope burns. Keeping this flame alive is a paramount task. We have to act as if a better future were possible, because if we do, it is. We can accomplish anything if we have hope. Hope is just another word for being connected to a purpose greater than ourselves. And when we are connected to Purpose, everything is possible.

THE CHALLENGE
Taming the Need to Win

———————

Competition is not in itself a bad thing; it is a natural and healthy part of life, allowing the best products and strategies to rise to the top for the benefit of all. Moreover, competition and cooperation are not directly opposed to one another. As a general rule, the best collaborators are also the most effective competitors.

But competition becomes dysfunctional when our competitive efforts are based on an "every person for themselves" mentality. This kind of competition doesn't necessarily allow the best to rise up, nor does it advance the best interests of the community.

For example, if members of the same sports team compete against each other to see who can get the most goals, the whole team may suffer as a result. The players will be thinking only of their own interests, not supporting what is best for the team. They may go so far as to sabotage each other in order to "win," even if this means that their team actually loses.

On the other hand, if the players are united in pursuit of a purpose greater than themselves, they will sacrifice individual recognition for the good of the team. Instead of each one trying to be the star, they will pass the ball so a teammate in a better position can score.

We cannot practice Cooperative Building while trying to win all the glory for ourselves. If I am compromising and brainstorming with others while secretly holding out hope that my name will be the one to go down in history for some revolutionary advance, I am not truly cooperating with the people around me. I am using them.

Comfortable with Mortality

As we go deeper in the practice of Cooperative Building, we recognize that we are cooperating not only with the people who are in our lives right now, but also with those who came before us, and even those yet to be born. We are part of a vast endeavor that started before we came into being and will continue long after we are gone.

Just as we must tame the need to win with regard to our peers, we must learn to accept that our generation will not be the ones to see this project through. Even if we did, we wouldn't deserve all the credit. If we are practicing Cooperative Building, that shouldn't matter to us. We want a new, more compassionate human community to emerge, whether or not we are remembered for our contribution. Like runners in a relay, we pass the baton to future generations.

In this way, Cooperative Building teaches us to become comfortable with our own mortality. The community we are seeking to co-create, this new way of living together, will not be completed by us in our lifetime, but the effects of our efforts will extend far beyond the span of our lives.

Recognizing this can help put our minds at ease as we confront the prospect of our own death. We can relax and let go, knowing that the universe is guiding the process, and that our actions are never in vain so long as they accord with this synergistic movement. Belonging to a Purpose greater than ourselves gives us the freedom to add our portion to a project that has been unfolding for generations, and will continue to unfold for countless more: creating a truly cooperative future for our descendants.

When we approach the task in this way, we become like the builders of great, ancient temples that took generations to complete. The grand venture we are engaged in did not originate with us, nor will we be the ones to finish it. We will not be present to witness the final result. But we can already see the outline of what is starting to take shape. If we use our imagination, we can even picture what it will look like when it is completed. We can catch a glimpse of a new reality that is beginning to emerge even now.

THE PRACTICE IN PRACTICE
Let's Figure This Out Together

———————

Power struggles are especially common in relationships between parents and children. Parents often think they know better than their children and want to make decisions for them, while children are eager to escape the influence of their parents and do things their own way. Parents do have a responsibility to make rules and set limits for their children's protection and safety. But in order to facilitate their healthy development and growth, parents also have to start letting go of control as the children grow older and allowing them to make their own choices. As a parent, I have to admit this can be agonizing to do. But cultivating a yielding and flexible mindset can help build resiliency into our relationships with our children as they make the transition from adolescence into adulthood.

For instance, say I have a daughter, my oldest child, who is seventeen years old and a senior in high school. She recently started her first serious romantic relationship, and our dynamic has begun to change. My daughter and I have always had very open communication, but lately she has become secretive and guarded. She lowers her voice abruptly while talking on the phone when I enter the room, and she doesn't tell me much about where she goes or who she's with. She has also started staying out late at night, violating her curfew on a more than a few occasions. Even more worrisome to me, her homework seems to be slipping. Although she has always been an excellent student, her most recent progress report indicates that she is not passing a couple of her classes.

One evening, she stays out all night without telling me, returning in the early hours of the morning. She goes straight to her room without offering any explanation for her behavior. It's the last straw. I am furious, but I am also feeling really scared. I suspect she and her boyfriend may have started having sex, though she hasn't told me this. I am really afraid she might get pregnant, drop out of high school, and not go on to college as she has always planned.

One response to this behavior would be to "grab the wheel." I could decide that, since my daughter clearly doesn't know any better, I have to exercise good judgment on her behalf. I might clamp down, ground her and prevent her from going out at night. I could also demand that she stop seeing her new boyfriend. This will almost certainly end up in a power struggle. My daughter could become even more secretive, and our relationship could deteriorate further as a result. I might lose the opportunity to be a person of influence in her life at a critical moment in her development.

Another strategy would be to adopt a cooperative approach to the problem. I could make an effort to offer help respectfully, in a way that doesn't take away my daughter's decision-making power. This might make it easier for her to receive help gracefully instead of resisting.

I could start by saying something like this: "You are practically an adult, and very soon you're going to be making all your own choices. I want you to be successful in school and in life. I have my own ideas about what's best for you, but I can't make you do things my way. How can we work together on this?"

I could try being creative and flexible. For example, I could negotiate a later curfew on weekends in return for more focus on schoolwork during the week.

Even if I think it would be better if she waited to start having sex, I could offer to help set up an appointment with her doctor to talk about birth control. Instead of trying to reassert control of the situation and make decisions for her, I can help her learn how to make smart, healthy choices for herself as she transitions into adulthood.

The Cooperative Workplace

The practice of Cooperative Building is essential to cultivating a healthy workplace environment with a strong team spirit. When we experience a sense of safety with our coworkers, we feel comfortable playing with new ideas and trying out different approaches. This enhances cohesion and creativity, and increases productivity and problem-solving on the job.

In the absence of these kinds of cooperative processes, however, a rigid, top-down structure tends to prevail. An authoritarian atmosphere stifles creativity and squelches important insights. The best leaders are usually not those who override their team members and stubbornly go it alone. Rather, they ask others for help and are willing to accept their input and advice, even if it is not what they want to hear. Sometimes, this can even prevent disastrous outcomes from occurring.

Here's an example of what Cooperative Building looks like in the workplace.

Let's say I am a senior executive leading a team that is just about to unveil a major new project. We've been working on the project for over a year now, and we're on the cusp of going live. The team is gathered for a final meeting to run through a checklist before the launch of the project. It's basically a dress rehearsal before lifting the curtain. There is a feeling of excitement in the air; the room crackles with energy. Everyone is enthusiastic, eager to get the project off the ground.

Unexpectedly, in the middle of the meeting, a junior associate who is new to the team raises a concern. The issue seems relatively minor, even trivial, but there is a small risk that if certain factors don't line up as expected, the entire project could be jeopardized. In order to address the concern, we would have to delay the launch of the project by a month, maybe more.

As the team leader, my immediate response is to quash the objection. The risk appears remote, and if we press ahead it seems likely that it will never materialize. This associate is new to the team and still quite junior. I think to myself, "How dare you think you know better than us? What could you possibly have picked up on that we missed?" If I am honest with myself, however, I would have to admit that I am nervous about losing face in front of my team. I don't want people to think I could have overlooked a potential threat to the project. I am afraid of looking weak and ineffective as a leader.

My team is looking to me for a signal how to respond. The first thing I do is to remind myself that this person is not an enemy, but an ally on the project. I take a breath and make a conscious effort to relax into the tension I am feeling. Then, I ask the associate to explain the risk in more detail. I try the idea on for size: what if this person is right? What if the risk factors did align this way? Then I put it to the team.

At first, everyone is silent. But finally one other person admits to having thought of the same thing. This person, who has been with the project since day one, confesses to having brushed off the concern because no one else on the team seemed to be worried about it. Others chime in that they hadn't foreseen this particular risk factor, but agree that it makes sense to investigate it. Soon the room is buzzing with conversations about how to address this newly-identi-fied challenge.

In the end, we decide to postpone the launch of the project. And that turns out to be a very good thing. During the extra month we take to address the concern, it becomes apparent that the risk was greater than we thought. We launch the project six weeks later, and it deploys without a hitch. In the months to come, we all attribute the success of the project to what happened in the meeting that day. Much of the credit deservedly goes to the junior associate, who gets a promotion shortly thereafter. But surprisingly (at least to me), people also credit my leadership with saving the project. My team expresses appreciation to me for being the kind of leader who would listen to the concerns of a junior associate and be willing to take them seriously. Far from looking weak as a leader as I had feared, people describe my actions that day as inspired and courageous leadership.

THE FINAL STEP
Integrating the Six Practices

If you've practiced incorporating each of the Six Spiritual Practices into your daily life as you read, I have no doubt you already have stories to share. Each practice is a powerful tool for infusing your days with intentionality, healthy relationships, and connection to Purpose.

Your challenge now is to integrate the Six Practices cohesively into your life, ingrain the mantras in your memory, and cultivate new habits so the practices come naturally as you meet new challenges.

I've been living with these practices for years, but it took a long time to find the right rhythm and get into the habit of naturally defaulting to them in challenging situations.

Let's take a look at an ordinary Wednesday in my life—not because I think you should do exactly what I do, but because it might spark some ideas.

A Day with the Six Practices

I start each day by saying the six mantras quietly to myself. Ideally, I take a moment to sit at the edge of my bed, relax my body, and run through all six mantras:

I accept everything I see.
I hear what my heart is saying.
I honor the boundaries I set.
I share what I have freely.
I receive the gift that is offered.
I co-create a new reality.

But let's be honest—mornings aren't always the most peaceful time of day. I have a young child in the house, and she gets up pretty early. There are many days when I simply say the six mantras in my head while brushing my teeth or getting dressed. This particular Wednesday was a mantras-while-teeth-brushing kind of day.

Using the mantras together in this way is like going through a checklist. When a pilot and co-pilot are preparing for takeoff, they run down a pre-flight checklist to ensure they haven't forgotten anything.

Saying the mantras one after the other is a way of making sure I have all the tools I need for the coming day.

I rode the bus to work that morning, and one of the passengers was being a little loud and unruly. It made me tense, so I put Compassionate Seeing to work. I started by saying the mantra quietly to myself (*I accept everything I see*), then I engaged a discovery mindset and asked myself, "I wonder what it's like to be you right now? What steps on your life's journey have brought you here?" As I imagined his experience, my irritation faded away.

As soon as I got to work, I wrote an invitation list as an exercise in Intentional Welcoming. I took a moment to ask, "Where do I choose to focus time, energy, and attention today?" Then, I wrote down a short list of high-level strategic priorities, which included a personal goal of supporting my physical health.

I'm not naturally great at paying attention to my emotions. It's easy for me to get caught up in the task at hand. So, to help me practice Heartfelt Listening throughout the day, I set a timer on my phone. When the timer goes off every two hours, I pause for a moment and ask myself, "What am I feeling?" and "What is this feeling telling me?" Then, I do a quick scan of my body to see what sensations I notice. On this Wednesday, I noticed I was feeling some tension between my shoulders, which is often a sign of stress. Then, I gave a name to what I was feeling: fear. I felt afraid that I wouldn't have time to get everything done and that other people would be upset with me. I said the mantra *I hear what my heart is saying* to acknowledge that I received the message.

In the late morning, the woman who sat next to me received a phone call that clearly upset her. Noticeably flustered, she asked for my advice. She needed to pick up her daughter from school, but also needed to wrap up a report that was due by noon. I thought I could add finishing her report to my to-do list without too much trouble. Before I offered, I quickly ran the idea through the two gates of Joyful Sharing in my head. Did I feel obligated to help her? No. Did I expect her to do something for me or behave a certain way if I offered to help? No. All good. I didn't want to feel any resentment later. I said the mantra *I share what I have freely* in my head, then told her not to worry, that I would finish her report. My gift meant so much to her, and I felt really happy about my decision.

At lunchtime, a few colleagues invited me to go across the street for fast food. Remembering my commitment to supporting my health, I decided to pass. Instead, I opted for a salad from a nearby café. Before eating, I paused for a moment to say the fifth mantra, *I receive the gift that is offered*. I use this as a way to express my gratitude for the gifts of the earth that sustain my life. Given that the salad had grilled chicken, I also gave thanks for the life of the animal. Afterwards, I took a walk outside, saying the same mantra to myself from time to time. I expressed appreciation for the beauty of sunlight glinting through tree leaves and for the joyous sight of a young boy playing with a dog. When my Heartfelt Listening timer went off, I noticed the tension I was feeling earlier had left.

That afternoon, I had a meeting I'd been dreading for days. The project to be discussed had been a sore spot with the team, and there were a lot of different ideas about which direction to pursue. One particularly challenging coworker and I had been butting heads on this for weeks. Before entering the room, I said the sixth mantra, *I co-create a new reality*. That brief reminder of Cooperative Building helped me lean into the tension with my colleague and enjoy the process of finding compromise.

When I got home that night, I had a hard time disconnecting from work. I was still thinking about the meeting, wondering if emails were being exchanged about it after hours. However, I wanted to prioritize time with my family, so I said the mantra *I honor the boundaries I set* and focused on my daughter's bedtime routine. As we sang a song together before bed, a precious time like no other, I silently whispered to myself, *I receive the gift that is offered*.

I always pause before bed to run through all six mantras—just like I do in the morning. I think of this as reconciling the day. Just as I might go through my bank account to look for discrepancies, I am checking for gaps between my intention and my actions. Without judging myself or anyone else, I ask, "Did I apply the practices when I wanted to today? Were there any situations where I would use one or more of these practices if I could do it over?" I'm careful not to be hard on myself in this process. I practice Compassionate Seeing, accepting the day and my responses for what they were. The key is to be consistent and keep making an effort every day.

The evening can also be a good time to write out a gratitude short list. I try to do this on Wednesdays because it's the middle of the work week and I sometimes start feeling overwhelmed with tasks. I wrote down a few things I was thankful for, including sweet bedtime routines with my daughter and colleagues who challenge me, and whispered "thank you" to the universe. That night, I also set a reminder to tell my difficult colleague that I appreciated the way he looked at our project from a totally different angle. For me, this gratitude exercise provides a sense of peace before I rest, and infuses my week with thankfulness.

Building a Community of Support

If you're serious about integrating the Six Spiritual Practices into your life for the long haul, I strongly encourage you to invite friends and family into the journey with you. The best way to deepen your practice is to do it with others. A community of support creates encouragement and gentle accountability for all involved. You can learn from others who have gone through similar experiences, and you can also share your own wisdom and insights.

One way to do this is to start a reading group. Meet regularly—maybe once a week or once a month—and work your way through this book together. I'd suggest tackling one practice at a time. A reading guide is available at www.sixpractices.com to help you dive deeper with this kind of community support group. In my experience, gathering regularly with a group like this is a perfect opportunity to further the creation of a new human community.

A Final Intention

Engaging the Six Practices is the most significant contribution you or I can make to creating a better world. Through these practices, we blossom into our full human potential.

As you integrate the practices into your daily life, you will feel yourself align with the flow of the universe. Although you may encounter resistance on the path, you will also find yourself supported in a thousand ways. You are practicing not just for yourself and those around you. You are part of a universal movement, an emerging new reality.

People in your life will notice the changes in you and become curious. In a cooperative way, without imposing anything on anyone, you will be able to share the gifts of renewed energy and clarity you have discovered through your connection to Purpose. You will become a force for good in the world, a source of inspiration for people all around you. This is my hope for you.

I'll close with a final intention, my own version of the elder's blessing from Part Four:

May reading this book bring you
as much inspiration and spiritual growth
as writing it has brought to me.